(Un)Manly
Citizens

LORI JO MARSO

(Un)Manly Citizens

*Jean-Jacques Rousseau's
and Germaine de Staël's
Subversive Women*

·

The
Johns Hopkins
University Press
*Baltimore &
London*

© 1999 The Johns Hopkins University Press
All rights reserved. Published 1999
Printed in the United States of America
on acid-free paper
2 4 6 8 9 7 3 1

The Johns Hopkins University Press
2715 North Charles Street
Baltimore, Maryland 21218-4363
www.press.jhu.edu

Library of Congress Cataloging-in-Publication Data
will be found at the end of this book.
A catalog record for this book is available
from the British Library.

ISBN 0-8018-6032-6

CONTENTS

•

PREFACE

—•—

Depictions of love always make a greater impression than the maxims of wisdom. —JEAN-JACQUES ROUSSEAU, *Letter to D'Alembert*

If we trust Rousseau in his conviction that love is a more powerful force than wisdom, we must seriously consider his own words about love. Rousseau wrote works in which love is painted in its most passionate, urgent, touching moments, only to be defeated in the name of reason and good sense at the hands of the virtuous society. As a consequence of love's defeat, women die and men lose their bearings as moral agents. Rousseau's men are transformed into "manly" citizens trained to obey the dictates of virtue and the demands of gender; his women, as remainder, are easily forgotten.

Or are they? As a writer with a tragic vision, Rousseau leaves one with nagging questions and unresolved dilemmas. Famous for his attempts to explore the paradoxes at the heart of the social contract (individual / community, freedom / equality, family / polity), Rousseau created "solutions" that come easily only at the expense of women.

My fascination with Rousseau's women motivates this book. Though Rousseau claims that in the best polity only men can be citizens, his men fail to be good citizens in almost every aspect. At the same time, Rousseau's women consistently demonstrate the qualities a good citizen needs. They show uncanny ability to integrate conflicting loyalties in their lives, they comprehend and act on particular interests without neglecting universal duties, and they expressly demonstrate good judgment in making decisions that affect their loved ones as well as the whole community.

Germaine de Staël is transfixed by Rousseau's tragic vision as she takes in the drama of the revolutionary politics surrounding her. Captivated by what she sees as Rousseau's sympathetic depiction of his women characters, and engulfed in revolutionary debates over the sexual politics of citizenship, Staël focuses her work on women in a visionary attempt to map the perils of ignoring the voices of the marginalized and excluded. She wisely reasons that although the Revolution promised equality and freedom, women who sought to extend these rights to themselves were vilified and forsaken. She articulates a criticism of unitary visions of the political good from women's perspective at the margins.

In the pages that follow, I will engage with Rousseau and Staël in my attempt to construct an alternative vision of citizenship. This alternative considers recognition of feminine difference to be central to democratic politics. The lives of these fictional women demonstrate the risks involved and the results incurred when we adopt a political vision willing to claim difference as pejorative and to banish the critical and the passionate from the political arena. Rousseau labels the subversive element at the heart of orderly and consensual politics as feminine, blaming women as passion's agents. Yet if Rousseau finds love and women to be such radically destructive forces, why does he depict both with such provocative charm and enduring seduction? Is there more to Rousseau's women, and Staël's attraction to these women, than meets the eye?

Situated as a late-twentieth-century feminist, I bring a number of questions and insights to these works that were not on the minds of either Rousseau or Staël. I will interrogate their works from a philosophical perspective that finds seemingly incidental questions of the location and desire of the feminine subject to be of dramatic importance for women's relationship to citizenship and women's potential to transform democratic politics as we now know it. Yet though I ask new questions of these authors, I also remain committed to their own preoccupations. Working with these texts over a period of years, I have come to believe that as modern authors anticipating, living, and evaluating the French Revolution's dilemmas of freedom, equality, sexuality, citizenship, and social order, Rousseau and Staël ask questions that are more than ever, and more urgently than ever, our own questions as well.

ACKNOWLEDGMENTS

·

About seven drafts and four years ago, this book was a dissertation. My longing to transgress the disciplinary boundaries between philosophy and literature, political science and storytelling, would have been met with disdain and pity, if not outright contempt, in many political science departments. This might have also been the case in New York University's politics department, were it not for the wonderfully open, intellectually daring souls who encouraged me in my blind but intuitive wanderings. Bertell Ollman, Christine Harrington, H. Mark Roelofs, and Timothy Mitchell deserve my heartfelt gratitude for creating a rare atmosphere that encouraged my intellectual creativity and growth.

Though they were completely unaware of their intervention at critical moments, Benjamin Barber, Patrick Riley, and Christine di Stefano provided sympathetic and constructive comments on the Staël chapters. Their comments and support gave me the courage I needed to continue to send out this work, previously rejected as "overly abstract" by historical journals, "too historical" by philosophy journals, and "too literary" by political science journals. As I prepared myself for a very abbreviated career after having fallen through all the disciplinary cracks, Robert Goodin revived my hopes by helping me to sharpen and focus my argument in the Delphine chapter for publication in the *Journal of Political Philosophy* 5, no. 2 (June 1997). I thank him for his generosity at a crucial moment and for the rights to reproduce this piece in a revised form here as Chapter 4. I am also grateful to Henry Tom from Johns Hopkins University Press for encouraging my work on this manuscript and supporting me through all its stages.

At my first job in San Antonio, Texas, I benefited from friendships with a core of appreciative and diverse students, colleagues, and friends willing to read parts of my manuscript. Jim Henson, Victoria Wohl, and Rodolfo Rosales deserve special thanks for sustaining me during the many rounds of revisions. Lita Bonciolini, Terry Kelley, Barbara Simerka, Steve Amberg, Arturo Vega, Tom Baylis, and Tami Waggonner also have my gratitude for friendship and intellectual camaraderie. Since then, in my move northeast to take a position at Union College in Schenectady, New York, I have encountered colleagues and friends to whom I have already incurred debts. I thank Charlotte Eyerman for suggesting Hersilia, featured in Jacques-Louis David's *Intervention of the Sabine Women* to represent the ultimate unmanly citizen on the book's cover. I thank Richard Fox for his collegiality and sense of humor.

Never formally trained in feminist theory, I have had to rely on the generosity of a number of feminist scholars who have graciously read my work, tolerated my many questions, and pushed my thinking and writing to its better forms. I thank Avriel Goldberger, Madelyn Gutwirth, and Anne A. A. Mini who, in the spirit of solidarity as scholars and friends, shared their expertise on Germaine de Staël. I especially thank Linda Zerilli and Lisa Disch for reading my work in various stages and extending me the kind of advice and confidence that allowed me to find my own voice as a feminist theorist. I also thank Elizabeth Mayes, René Marion, Margaret Moore, Jodi Dean, and Wendy Gunther-Canada for their friendship, conversations, and shared insights.

It would take pages to name the many people who influenced me during my many years of graduate school at the London School of Economics and NYU. These sister and fellow graduate students enriched my thinking and contributed to my knowledge in ways that are impossible to accurately map. I must single out Marla Brettschneider and Patricia Moynagh for remaining my closest friends over a period of many years. Together we learned about feminism and activism and made long lists of books to be read and ideas to be put into practice.

I owe my sanity and success to the patience and love of my family. I want to especially thank my parents, Jo and Tom Marso, for their emotional and financial support and for their understanding about my life and goals. My husband, Tom Lobe, has been a partner at every stage of the process this book has gone through from its dissertation days, to article submissions, to the final touches on the book. He has had to endure my many mood swings, my absences from family functions, and all that came with finishing this project while taking on more. Moreover, Tom's care in raising our children, Lucas and Luci, and maintaining our "family" in all its many manifestations made it possible for me to have the kind of time needed to think and write and begin a career. Tom suspended his own academic career to allow me to "have it all" (or at least agonize over how to "do it all") while our family stays together. Rousseau's and Staël's stories about women attest to the fact that it is impossible to measure the debts, sacrifices, loyalty, and gratitude inspired by love. I dedicate this book to Tom as a small token of the bond inspired by love and friendship.

A NOTE ON TRANSLATIONS

•

In an effort to make this book widely accessible to overlapping and inter-disciplinary audiences, whenever possible I have referred to English translations of French texts. See the list below for information on translations used and how reference to them is indicated throughout the chapters.

TEXTS AUTHORED BY JEAN-JACQUES ROUSSEAU

LD'A *Politics and the Arts: A Letter to M. D'Alembert on the Theatre*, translated by Allan Bloom (Glencoe, Ill.: Free Press, 1960).

SC *Social Contract and Discourses*, translated by G. D. H. Cole (London: Everyman's Library, 1973).

DI *Discourse on the Origins of Inequality*, translated by G. D. H. Cole (London: Everyman's Library, 1973).

Confessions *The Confessions* and *Correspondence*, including the *Letters to Malesherbes*, translated by Christopher Kelly, Roger D. Masters, and Peter G. Stillman (Hanover, N.H.: University Press of New England, 1995).

GP *The Government of Poland*, translated by Willmoore Kendall (Indianapolis: Bobbs-Merrill, 1972).

E *Emile, or On Education*, translated by Allan Bloom (New York: Basic Books, 1979). Cited in the text as E, Book:page number.

J *Julie, or the New Heloise*, translated and annotated by Philip Stewart and Jean Vaché (Hanover, N.H.: University Press of New England, 1997). Cited in the text as J, Part:Letter, page number.

ES   *Emile et Sophie, ou Les Solitaires,* Oeuvres Complètes, Vol. 4 (Paris: Gallimard, 1969). I thank Roger Hagedorn for his expertise in helping me to translate this piece.

TEXTS AUTHORED BY GERMAINE DE STAËL

LR   *Letters on Rousseau,* translated by Vivian Folkenflik, *An Extraordinary Woman: Selected Writings of Germaine de Staël* (New York: Columbia University Press, 1987).

EF   *Essay on Fictions,* translated by Vivian Folkenflik, 1987.

IP   *The Influence of the Passions on the Happiness of Individuals and Nations,* translated by Vivian Folkenflik, 1987.

OLF   *On Literature,* translated by Vivian Folkenflik, 1987

OLB   *On Literature,* translated by Morroe Berger, *Madame de Staël on Politics, Literature, and National Character* (Garden City, N.Y.: Doubleday, 1964).

CFR   *Considerations on the Principal Events of the French Revolution,* 3 vols. (London: Baldwin, Cradock, and Joy, 1818). Cited within the text as CFR, Part:Vol:Chapter, page number.

Q   *Réflexions sur le procès de la Reine, par une Femme,* Bibliothèque Nationale Librarie 3272 (August 1793). Unless otherwise indicated, all references to this work will be to the English translation by Anne A. A. Mini in "An Expressive Revolution: The Political Theory of Germaine de Staël" (Ph.D. diss., University of Washington, 1995), Appendix B, 365–92.

D   *Delphine,* translated by Avriel Goldberger (DeKalb: Northern Illinois University Press, 1995). Cited in the text as D, Part: Letter, page number.

CI   *Corinne, or Italy,* translated by Avriel Goldberger (New Brunswick, N.J.: Rutgers University Press, 1987). Cited in the text as CI, Book:Part, page number.

(Un)Manly
Citizens

1

Introduction

Imagining Woman

•

For him she is sex —absolute sex, no less. She is defined and differentiated with reference to man and not he with reference to her; she is the incidental, the inessential as opposed to the essential. He is the Subject, he is the Absolute—she is the Other.

—SIMONE DE BEAUVOIR, *The Second Sex*

The cave is the representation of something always already there, of the original matrix/womb which these men cannot represent since they are held down by chains that prevent them from turning their heads or their genitals toward the daylight.

—LUCE IRIGARAY, *Speculum of the Other Woman*

Simone de Beauvoir and Luce Irigaray argue that in the history of Western philosophy *Woman*[1] has been defined as an idealized essence that is merely a product of the male imagination, a fiction based in male desire. What we have learned about women from Western philosophy has really been a story of Woman: she is either man's other, man's mirror image, or she suffers from a complete failure of representation within the male symbolic. Within this history, there is a lack of knowledge about who women really are: feminists debate whether there is a feminine essence based in sex (which is not defined or constructed by men) or whether all sexual distinction is a product of gender.[2] Another way of posing these questions is to ask which kinds of characteristics (biological, historical, psychological, political, emotional, moral, constitutive) designate individual women as members of their sex, and who has the power over those definitions.

These questions lead to further questions: Does an identity as women (if we can define it) take precedence, in some or all instances, over other identities women may have? Must we advance Woman as a category in order to speak in the name of women, and what are the dangers of that definition?[3] How has women's exclusion from categories of self, citizen, and individual affected the way Woman has been constructed and the way women think of themselves? Does women's exclusion from these categories in itself portend transformative potential?[4] Once it has been argued that citizens should be "manly," and we recognize women's philosophical and political exclusion from this category, from which subjective position and in whose name should women engage in the work of "unmanning"?

I enter into this discussion over the construction of Woman through the works of Rousseau and Staël. I look to the construction of women's subjectivity in these authors as a way to ask questions about women's relationship to citizenship at a historical moment in which the questions of who should be a citizen and which kinds of qualities should be central to citizenship were highly contested. The designation of gender difference was key to the debate surrounding these questions. Like never before (and arguably never since), the intellectual atmosphere prior to and during the French Revolution encouraged a fundamental rethinking of politics, including women's potential role in the political sphere. The legacy of the French Revolution for women is subject to much debate.[5] That being a man was essential for being a citizen has been firmly established and documented by feminist authors.[6] Rousseau and Staël show evidence of this requirement: Rousseau theorizes the gender boundaries essential to citizenship, and Staël laments their political implications. However, whereas previous authors have commented on the "success" of Rousseau's theory in that his philosophy mandated the exclusion of women from politics, I will look at Rousseau's "failure." The success of Rousseau's male citizens (a very limited success, if even that) is had only in light of the demise of his women. Staël finds herself attracted to these very women in her own portrayal of women in work that promises to transform Enlightenment notions of political space, political deliberation, and ways to theorize the relationship between individual and community. In both authors, subversion of dominant conceptions of politics and the ideal of the "manly" citizen as central to those visions is possible only through recognition of feminine subjectivity.

Using the work of Rousseau and Staël, I will argue that feminine subjectivity was never fully foreclosed as outside of politics, as a complementary mirror of the male citizen. Rather, a subversive feminine subjectivity is contained at the core of the male self.[7] This self is never quite able to master the feminine, never quite able to displace or forget that which he cannot embrace in his quest to be a man. The women portrayed by Rousseau and Staël are internally subversive of the male citizen. At the same time, they exhibit qualities that gesture toward alternative conceptions of identity and of citizenship. The feminine presence in these works (and at the core of male subjectivity) simultaneously constitutes and unsettles the identity of the manly citizen, threatening to unman it at every turn.

Struggling with the Dictates of "Manly" Citizenship

It is possible that there are in the world a few women worthy of being listened to by a serious man; but, in general, is it from women that he ought to take counsel, and is there no way of honoring their sex without abasing our own?

—JEAN-JACQUES ROUSSEAU, *Letter to D'Alembert*

Ever since the Revolution men have deemed it politically and morally useful to reduce women to a state of the most absurd mediocrity.

—GERMAINE DE STAËL, *On Literature*

It seems clear that Rousseau recognized the subversive potential of women; Staël documents that the French Revolution took him seriously. Why does Rousseau consider "manliness" to be at stake when women speak? *What is so dangerous about what women do and say?* Women's "chatter" is so threatening that we dare not let women voice their ideas in public. Banished from the space where male citizens conduct their serious business, Woman is theorized as the ominous presence, the dangerous supplément, the remainder: she is the intermediate body against which the male citizen is defined, but she is easily and quickly forgotten.[8]

The effects of declaring women's deviation (or difference) from standards required for citizenship were, and continue to be, profound. As Joan Scott puts it: "[T]he word 'lie' echoed from one end of the nineteenth century to the other as feminists denounced the Revolution and the First, Second, and Third Republics for betraying the universal principles of liberty, equality, and fraternity by refusing citizenship to women."[9] Philosophically and politically, the Revolution left in its wake a conception of citizenship that denied women their personhood by denying their right to participate in defining a collective future. Male subjectivity, played out in this case as a claim to political power to determine the kind of society in which we all will live, is seemingly predicated on female objectivity. Man looks to Woman to find a reflection of himself; Woman is entirely colonized and completely known. A prime example of this colonization, this knowing of Woman, comes out of the work of Rousseau. Sophie is consistently cited as *the* inessential woman.[10] Rousseau claims that Sophie is "made for man's delight." This oppressive system would seem closed and all-encompassing, a monument to the scope and power of a dominant ideology.

Yet women like Sophie were considered so dangerous to politics that they were denied the rights of citizenship in Rousseau's theory and in French revolutionary politics. What is it that women (even women created within an ideological system saturated by man's imagination of Woman) say, do, or threaten to say or do that is potentially subversive of the world that men have constructed and seek to maintain? In investigating this question, I assume that at the site of the creation of subjectivity there is a possibility for its subversion, that our understanding of ourselves and others is always in crisis. In my interpretation of Rousseau and Staël, both fully recognize that identities can never be firmly established. This will seem an unlikely reading of Rousseau, who is best known for fixing not only the identity of citizens but also the identities of man and woman as well.

Rousseau is best known as the spirit behind the French Revolution, the creator of the social contract, the theorist of republican identity. Born in Geneva, the son of a poor watchmaker whose mother died at his birth, Rousseau identified himself with the poor, the social misfits, and the marginalized. His condemnation of the excesses of the Old Regime posthumously earned his fame with the Jacobin revolutionaries, who interpreted Rousseau as articulating the virtue and spirit of the new male citizen who would create the new French Republic.

I will argue, however, that Rousseau's work reveals the futility of attempting to "fix" any identity, particularly those of citizen, man, and woman. Ironically, Rousseau worked with furious intensity to accomplish this impossible task. It is almost as if he fails to acknowledge his own insights into the ways in which our multiple selves cut against any effort to strictly identify ourselves as one kind of person. Rousseau's work makes clear that we all must deal with conflicting loyalties in our lives. Loyalty to love clashes with loyalty to marriage, commitment to family clashes with commitment to polity, original nature clashes with behavior in society, and amour-de-soi clashes with amour-propre. Rousseau sets up these oppositions as almost impossible to overcome. In *Emile* he argues that "forced to combat nature or the social institutions, one must choose between making a man or a citizen, for one cannot make both at the same time" (E, I:39).

Ironically, the way Rousseau attempts to solve the dilemma of humankind's conflicted nature is to make man and citizen simultaneously. Carole Pateman notes that the social contract is first a sexual contract whereby *man equals citizen*.[11] In other words, Rousseau chooses to enact strict gender boundaries in order to secure his social contract. Having seen no evidence for sexual difference in nature, Rousseau opts to create and enforce sexual difference through education to guarantee what he sees as the proper functioning of society. He builds an excessively univocal model of the social contract, one in which everyone must speak in the same (male) voice in order to be heard. In his attempt to forge a new basis for society, Rousseau decrees that through an act of will, men must turn themselves into citizens able to deny personal loyalties and place all emotional investment in the fatherland. Rousseau's women, confined to the safety of the private sphere, sacrifice for their men and children. This is the Rousseau feminists have often criticized as offering a truncated version of Woman defined in the male image. This is also the Rousseau that, Carol Blum tells us, the Jacobins found to be of such great inspiration in creating the new French Republic.[12]

I maintain, however, that Rousseau's constructed gender boundaries fail to buttress, and ultimately serve to undermine, his social contract. This is evident when one closely studies the women he created. In *Emile et Sophie, ou Les Solitaires,* and in *La Nouvelle Héloïse,* Rousseau's heroines, Sophie and Julie, end up dead for the sake of a community that fails to prosper in their absence. When feminist scholars study the death of Rousseau's heroines, the patriarchal characteristics of the general will and the excessive passion of the women who fail to "fit" these conditions are noted.[13] Though Rousseau went to great lengths to expound on the dangers that undomesticated (sexual, theatrical, unchaste) women pose to the virtuous social and political order, to assume that Rousseau was willing to eliminate women simply in order for the social contract to work is to assume, *against* Rousseau, that the demands of virtue and the well-being of society is a more compelling and convincing good than is the passion of lovers and our attachments to particular individuals. Given Rousseau's sympathies with his women characters and the delicacy and strength he puts forth to portray them, I am *not* willing to assume Rousseau's satisfaction with the outcome for his women.[14] It might even be the case that Rousseau's heroines die precisely in order for us to lament such a fate. The good society he creates is not worth the sacrifice of women like Sophie and Julie.

Consider Rousseau's warnings against Racine's play, *Bérénice,* in his *Letter to D'Alembert.* Rousseau argues that the audience is initially disposed to find Titus's incessant wavers "between his mistress and his duty" as "effeminate" complaints unworthy of his character. By the end of the play, however, the spectator "ends up pitying this sensitive man whom he despised, by being concerned with the same passion which he considered criminal, by secretly *grumbling* at the sacrifice he is forced to make for the laws of his country" (LD'A, 52–53, emphasis added). Moreover, when Bérénice, the lover, is sent away so that Titus can fulfill his duty, this dutiful outcome "does not erase the effect of the play. . . . Titus can very well remain a Roman; he is the only one on his side; all the spectators have married Bérénice" (LD'A, 53).

In taking seriously Rousseau's belief that the passions of love are more convincing than the demands of duty, I will argue that an alternative interpretation of Rousseau's work is located in the perspective of the women characters he creates in his novels. When we study Rousseau from the standpoint of these women, a radically different Rousseauian political philosophy comes into view. Rousseau's women undermine his vision of manly citizenship; these women are not merely a male reflection, nor do they serve to reinforce a feminine essence. Rather, when we, as readers, identify and sympathize with the fate of these women, we are encouraged to recognize a radical feminine difference that opens up an alternative democratic future.

This is a Rousseau left mostly unexplored by feminist political theorists.[15] I look to Rousseau's women, primarily Sophie and Julie, in order to trace Rousseau's ambivalence about constructing gender difference in terms of the male model and as the primary signifier for claims upon rights and responsibilities of citizenship. Through a careful study of the women characters in Rousseau's work, I sketch the early contours of an alternative conception of citizenship, one that recognizes the subversive potential of Rousseau's women. The conception of citizenship suggested by the feminine presence in Rousseau acknowledges radical difference: Rousseau's women implicitly condemn the unitary public that Rousseau works so hard to achieve. In an attempt to voice the implications of their own exclusion, their gestures and practice sketch a politics unable to be consumed by the male imagination. This is a politics built on the art of sociability, the value of civil conversation, sensitivity to diversity, and the necessity of engaging with radically different perspectives. If we take Rousseau's women seriously, his work is rich with possibility for feminist theory.

At least one woman did take Rousseau seriously: Germaine de Staël. Staël publicly identified Jean-Jacques Rousseau as her inspiration, mentor, and muse. Staël's first major publication, the one that established her as a writer with great promise, was her *Considerations on the Writing and Character of Jean-Jacques Rousseau* (1788). In this work, Staël praises Rousseau's keen knowledge of women's hearts. She is inexorably drawn to Rousseau's portrayal of his heroines' art of loving. Staël builds on Rousseau's model of femininity, but they part ways on at least one crucial matter: Staël refuses to endorse the strict gender boundaries that Rousseau sees as crucial to the smooth functioning of the polity, as integral in identifying who is to be a citizen, and as the determining factor for modeling Woman and citizen as exclusive categories.

Daughter of Jacques Necker, popular finance minister on the eve of the French Revolution, and Suzanne Necker, prominent *salonnière* in Paris from 1766–1790, Staël was a first-hand witness to the various stages of the Revolution culminating in the reign of Napoleon. At the forefront of Staël's work was her growing awareness that to be a woman in the new French Republic was to be a member of a newly contentious political category. After 1793 any attempts to include both women and men within the rhetorical language of the *Declaration of the Rights of Man and Citizen* were thwarted by a narrow Rousseauist interpretation of which gender (only the male) would have access to the rights and responsibilities of citizenship. With the publications of *Delphine* in 1802 and *Corinne, or Italy* in 1807, Staël entered the fray of revolutionary debate concerning which particular kinds of qualities and moral sensibilities define a good citizen. Within both novels she seeks to explain what went wrong with the 1789 Revolution, which had rejected the country's inegalitarian past but failed to adequately execute a future capable of protecting human liberty and dignity. Staël "endeavors to answer both Locke and Montesquieu's fear of arbitrary power and Rousseau's paranoia about the oppressive nature of any rule but self-rule."[16] In post-Jacobin France it became imperative to find a path beyond the liberal and republican models, a way to conceptualize citizenship that would protect the individual and also give meaning to the nation.

Staël builds on a buried yet central alternative within Rousseau's work that uncovers the radical potential of the feminine as a way to reconceptualize citizenship. Staël demonstrates the limits of establishing strict identities (in terms of gender, race, sexual preference, or any axis) in the construction of citizenship, seeking instead to draw a practice of democratic citizenship that is willing to recognize individuals in terms of their concrete histories and situations.

Drawing on much of Staël's oeuvre, yet concentrating on *Delphine* and *Corinne*, I will argue that Staël is able to take us much farther than Rousseau possibly could, moving to a theoretical framework beyond the conundrum of liberal versus communitarian models of citizenship,[17] equality versus difference in feminist theory.[18] Staël has no truck with either the liberal model of citizenship, which advances relations between strangers as the ideal for citizens, or the communitarian model, which tends to erase differences in advocating fraternal community. She warns that when we fail to think of our sister and fellow citizens as individual persons with loving ties to family and friends, it is far too easy to disregard the rights of individuals (especially extraordinary individuals[19]) in the name of an unspecified freedom for each or as sacrifice for the good of the whole. As Staël argues:

> Once one can imagine the possibility of making an innocent suffer, perhaps for many centuries to come, it becomes atrocious to enact such [a law], even for the good of an entire nation. The frightful alternatives, on the other hand, are almost never couched at all in terms of real effects. The truths of a certain order are at once counseled by reason and inspired by the heart: it is almost always in the interests of politics to listen to pity; but in that forum, cruelty, not pity, all too often has the last word, and as Machiavelli, in his own code of tyranny, said, *it is necessary to know how to attack those whom one cannot make perish.*[20]

This statement illustrates a fundamental principle that guides Staël's political philosophy: were we to know that laws constructed in terms of the general good brought about the suffering of individual persons, we would never be willing to endorse such laws. It is clear that Staël would never endorse the most (in)famous precept of *The Social Contract*, namely that for the good of the whole we must sometimes force people to be free (SC, 195). Rousseau's own work fosters our suspicion of such rigid principles in demonstrating the devastating effects that this "forcing" of the community will has on particular women.

It is instructive that in the quote above, Staël contrasts pity to cruelty and advances pity as a *political* principle. In rejecting the need to choose between models based on the "right" (presuming obligatory respect and dignity for strangers) and the "good" (presuming moral/political consensus amongst all in pursuit of higher goals), Staël argues that when pity is eradicated, cruelty takes root. In her analysis, pity is a political and emotional attribute that allows us to see sister and fellow citizens beyond the false choice of either the stranger (the other) or the familiar (the self). Pity is what enables us to see citizens as individuals defined by their own subjective vision—as people with particular attributes and loving ties. Herein lies the core notion of the kind of alternative politics that I have derived from my reading of Staël. Though the liberal model, based on conceptions of right, claims to protect individual freedoms, and though the communitarian model, based on conceptions of good, claims the strength of consensus, my interpretation of Staël's work suggests that we must reject both models. Because neither model is willing to examine the context in which the individual lives, works, and loves, neither adequately protects the individual who challenges public opinion.

Staël notices that women are the ones who most constantly challenge public opinion in the period of the French Revolution, demanding that rights of citizenship be extended to all. She focuses on women's exclusion from citizenship in order to highlight the philosophical dilemma at hand. Staël's work reveals that when we adopt the vantage point of women excluded from the new French Republic's category of citizen, we simultaneously are able to criticize and envision. This vantage point reveals the problems inherent in manly citizenship while pointing toward ways to unman that vision. Women's exclusion from politics, in this historical instance, points us toward a new model for citizenship that challenges Enlightenment models of liberalism and communitarianism.

The way in which Staël recognizes and embraces the feminine presence can be theorized as an alternative that cannot be contained by present categories of politics or gender difference. Staël finds that women, socialized to consider more fully the effects of general laws on friends and family, are more willing to acknowledge others unlike themselves and to consider the perspectives of those with whom they might disagree. Another way of saying this is to argue that women do not fit very well into a polity that calls upon us to interact as strangers according mutual respect (but only that), nor do women fit into the unitary public. Following upon Rousseau's emphasis on empathy, Staël looks to the concept of pity (defined as a recognition of the ways in which an other is both like and unlike ourselves) and the ways in which women exercise pity as an alternative ground for forging communal consensus while protecting individuals.

Certain problems arise as distinct to the project of advocating an emotion, such as pity or love, as a political principle, and there are notable and persuasive objections to such a proposal. I will discuss these problems and objections throughout, discerning and evaluating Staël's response to them in Chapter 4.[21] Drawing on and extending Rousseau's and Staël's insights, I will argue that the alternative democratic practice suggested by the women they portray emphasizes the importance of consciousness-raising, open forums for discussion, face-to-face decision making that undermines rather than buttresses the simple "reading" of a transparent other, nonhierarchical power structures, and the building of consensus whereby we do not force others to be free. Such a democratic practice teaches us that as citizens, we must be able to do more than rationally assert our self-interest (as liberal selves who relate as strangers) or submit to the general will (in terms of either a masculine heroism or feminine intimacy).

Instead, we must democratically participate. Rousseau's and Staël's women gesture toward a version of participatory citizenship that does not make the typical communitarian mistake of sacrificing individual liberty and obscuring individual visions. Because these women have themselves been marginalized and silenced by their political communities, their actions suggest a sensitivity to retaining the goals of respect for diverse individuals within a community in which all contribute. This alternative recognizes that as ever-changing selves with conflicting loyalties and varying perspectives, we come together in a democratic polity in an ongoing process of recognizing others both like and unlike ourselves, engaging in public debate in terms of our diverse needs and identities, and proceeding to govern ourselves despite the difficulty of the process. This kind of democratic practice is rooted, for both Rousseau and Staël, in recognizing women's desire.

Rousseau's and Staël's Methodology: Telling Persuasive Stories

> If a speech could be purely present, unveiled, naked, offered up in person in its truth, without the detours of a signifier foreign to it, if at the limit an undeferred *logos* were possible, it would not seduce anyone.
> —JACQUES DERRIDA, *Dissemination*

The way Rousseau and Staël choose to investigate intellectual questions is clearly integral to their politics. One of the most salient features in their work is that both Rousseau and Staël suggest that the capacity for judgment emerges from and through the emotions. The emotions are aroused through erotic desire, sympathy with and connection to others, and/or activating the imagination. Neither succumbs to the dogma that truth must be found through philosophy's usual methods: reducing the other to the same, reducing difference to similarity, making sure that all the parts fit into the whole, charting some sort of organization through chaos, and displacing emotion in the quest for a sanitized reason. For Rousseau and Staël, thinking and judging, both political and moral, are ways of understanding the world best enabled through feeling, direct experience, or imagination if direct experience is unavailable.

In his *Confessions,* Rousseau admits that he "felt before thinking" (I:7). He learned to understand everything through his senses and emotions first, factored through reason only later. It is the direct experience of suffering an injustice (for example, being accused, though innocent, of breaking one of Mlle. Lambercier's combs) that teaches the young Jean-Jacques to understand the ways of the world and sympathize with those who suffer (Confessions, I:16–17). Likewise, imagination plays an integral role in judgment. As Rousseau puts it: "It is imagination which extends for us the measure of the possible, whether for good or bad, and which consequently excites and nourishes the desires by the hope of satisfying them" (E, II:81). Reason, which guides our choices, is, for Rousseau, originally born of desire and imagination.

Staël also emphasizes the role that feelings play in nurturing our ability to make good political and moral choices. She writes that "man has only two distinct faculties: reason and imagination . . . man's most valuable faculty is his imagination" (EF, 60–61). Like Rousseau, Staël claims that the way to change moral and political ideas is through the heart. Banishing the passions as philosophies of deliberative justice suggest is considered a travesty by Staël. She clarifies: "Some severe philosophers condemn all emotions, wanting moral authority to rule by a simple statement of moral duty. . . . Nothing is less suited to human nature" (EF, 74).

Throughout her oeuvre, Staël develops the idea that emotional commitments to particular others are essential to consider in making decisions that affect us all. Staël would never approve of the Rawlsian veil of ignorance whereby each individual must be denied crucial information about family, loyalties, and social position in order to negotiate rationally and fairly concerning the general good. Staël proposes instead that a viable human conception of rational self-interest and duty to community is integrally connected to the happiness of particular and identifiable others, that individual happiness as tied to the good of others, in fact, inspires community spirit. She writes, for example, that "general truths . . . are made up of *every fact* and *every individual being*" (OLB, 247), that to banish love/eros/passion from the public sphere is an act by "atrocious men" attempting to "simplify their calculations [of politics] by omitting suffering, feeling, and imagination" (OLB, 247).

Despite their interest in political philosophy, Rousseau and Staël were willing to engage, and indeed embrace, their fascination with domestic life, erotic love, and passion, and its literary forms: the novel, poetry, elliptical texts. In the works that I will be discussing in the following four chapters, Rousseau and Staël depart from conventional philosophical prose in order to experiment with ways of discussing the complexity of politics that are more attentive to particular details, layers of meaning, and the surprising varieties of identities and ways of knowing. Each author tells a story or stories, and in doing so is able to discuss politics at the level of the personal, the passionate, the erotic. They encourage us to identify with their characters. In Rousseau's work, we get to know Emile, Sophie, St. Preux, Julie, Claire, Wolmar, and, in his own *Confessions,* Rousseau himself. In Staël's work, the same is true: we identify with Delphine and her dilemma, Corinne and her aspirations. Even when they are writing in the more conventional manner of political philosophy, the personal slips in. Rousseau and Staël both take for granted that their own personal quirks and knowledge of love are relevant in discussing the best way of organizing political life.

The commitment of Rousseau and Staël to emotion and to the forms of exposition it inspires leads me to take seriously the alternative kinds of texts they write, particularly the novel and its contribution to authoritative claims in the field of political philosophy.[22] Lisa Disch has written that "under certain conditions, a story can be a more powerful critical force than a theoretical analysis . . . a well-crafted story shares with the most elegant theories the ability to bring a version of the world to light that so transforms the way people see that it seems never to have been otherwise."[23] Philosophy has long been associated with the quest for universal truths, whereas literature is associated with attention to detail. Yet the opposition is often drawn too boldly. Aristotle wisely notes that "intelligence is about *human concerns*, about what is open to deliberation . . . it must also come to know particulars, since it is concerned with action and action is about particulars."[24] Martha Nussbaum reminds us of the political dimensions to this philosophy/literature dualism. She argues that certain kinds of truths have historically not been allowed to count as contributions to philosophical understanding: "[Philosophy] insists that the non-repeatable and sensuous aspects of the particular case are irrelevant, even a hindrance to correct seeing."[25] These unacceptable truths are most often told by women, by the marginalized and oppressed, by those whose languages and experiences do not directly correspond to the "rational truth" of political regimes. In focusing on women and the truths they tell in the novels that Rousseau and Staël write, I seek to make connections between the acknowledgment of women's desire, the way that desire disrupts any claims to fixed identities, and how this disruption challenges certain philosophical and political truths that deny the voices of those who fail to conform.

The Disruptive Desire of Rousseau's and Staël's Women

Each of the excerpts below recounts the early stages of a relationship between lovers: Sophie and Emile, Julie and St. Preux, Delphine and Léonce, Corinne and Oswald. In each, an acknowledgment of a woman's desire threatens to subvert the norms that govern masculinity and the rules that constitute male identity through a recognition that the woman is neither man's mirror opposite (the Other) nor a truncated version of the man (the Same). Each, I argue, is a gesture toward a genuine recognition of feminine sexual difference that is not measured in terms of men or in terms of masculine Western metaphysics. I will put each quote in its context in order to begin to articulate the outline of an alternative politics that moves beyond the unitary public constructed through male will and maintained through enforced gender boundaries articulated in terms of man as the measure.

The discussion turns to the travelers losing their way. "Sir," the master of the house says to him, "you appear to me to be a likable and wise young man, and that makes me think that you and your governor have arrived here tired and wet like Telemachus and Mentor on Calypso's island." "It is true," Emile answers, "that we find here the hospitality of Calypso." His Mentor adds, "And the charms of Eucharis." But although Emile knows the *Odyssey*, he has not read *Telemachus*. He does not know who Eucharis is. As for the girl, I see her blush up to her eyes, lower them toward her plate, and not dare to murmur . . . but in spite of this modest air and these lowered eyes, her tender heart palpitates with joy and tells her that Telemachus has been found. (Jean-Jacques Rousseau, *Emile, or On Education*)

While my heart is overflowing I must tell you a truth which it feels strongly and of which yours must persuade you: it is that in spite of fortune, of parents, and of ourselves, our destinies are forever united, and that we can no longer be happy or unhappy if not together. . . . Rid yourself therefore of the hope, if you ever entertained it, of finding individual happiness, and purchasing it at the expense of mine. . . . Believe me, my friend, I know your heart much better than you do. . . . I wish you could appreciate how much it matters to us both that you rely on me to look after our common destiny. . . . For me, the more I reflect on our situation, the more I find that reason asks of you what I ask of you in the name of love. (Jean-Jacques Rousseau, *La Nouvelle Héloïse*)

For a long time I spoke with him, in front of him, for him; my pleasure in this conversation was entirely new to me. Until then, I had thought of conversation only as a way of showing the breadth and subtlety of my ideas, but with Léonce, I looked for subjects more closely akin to the soul's affection; we talked about novels: one by one we covered those few which have probed the most secret griefs of sensitive characters. I felt a depth of emotion enliven all of my words: my quickened heartbeat did not abate even when our discussion turned purely on literature. My mind had retained ease and facility, but I felt my soul in turmoil, as in life's most important circumstances; and in the evening, I could not persuade myself that no extraordinary event had occurred around me. (Germaine de Staël, *Delphine*)

The senator took up the crown of myrtle and laurel he was to place on Corinne's head. She unwound the turban encircling her forehead, and all her ebony hair came tumbling in curls upon her shoulders. Bareheaded, she went forward, her gaze brightened by a sense of pleasure and gratitude she in no way sought to hide. Once more she knelt, this time to receive the crown, but she seemed more composed and less tremulous now. She had just spoken, filling her soul with the noblest thoughts, and through the power of enthusiasm she was not timid anymore. No longer a fearful woman, she was an inspired priestess, joyously devoting herself to the cult of genius. . . . Touched to the quick, Oswald came forward to speak to her, but he could not master the embarrassment holding him back. Corinne watched him closely for a time, careful not to draw his attention. (Germaine de Staël, *Corinne, or Italy*)

The first excerpt, from Book V of Rousseau's *Emile, or On Education,* recounts the moment when Sophie first realizes that Emile is the husband and lover for whom she has longed. We are accustomed to reading this passage (and indeed all of *Emile*) as part of a narrative whereby Emile (with the constant help and intervention of his tutor, Jean-Jacques) learns, through imagination, to desire the suitably educated natural woman. He consequently finds her, woos her, and conquers her. As is typical of most feminist interpretations of this text, Sarah Kofman sees the whole of *Emile* as the quintessential story of women's subordination:

> As a pedagogical novel, *Emile* sets out to re-create women so as to perfect and improve upon divine creation. An appropriate education, one in conformity with nature, should beget the sort of woman who can now only be found in some mythical natural preserve, untouched by civilization—a wise and perfect woman, Sophie, a woman who knows how to stay within the limits Nature has assigned to her, in the place befitting her sex, subordinate to man, the one and only king of creation.[26]

We are also told, however, that arranging this hierarchy between men and women is not as easy as it sounds. For in Rousseau's oeuvre, women have a "natural" power over men whereby women use their sexuality in such a way that men are unable, in the face of these erotic temptations, to control their desire. Susan Okin explains that "this tremendous sexual power over man was what made him [Rousseau] so adamant that women should not, in addition, 'usurp men's rights,' or, in other words, make themselves the equals of men in those other areas which men have traditionally reserved for themselves."[27] As these readings go, the only power that Rousseau accords to women is that of her ability to arouse men's desire; Rousseau finds this single power so dangerous that he is unwilling to give women equal political rights or equal status in the family. In these accounts, Woman is only seen through male desire. Responsible for dangerously arousing man's passions, Woman must be controlled and reined in through a process of domestication.

There is much evidence within Rousseau's work to buttress this version of the feminist interpretation. When we read, for example, that Sophie's education is to be directed solely toward pleasing her future mate or that Julie and St. Preux must deny their love for each other because Julie's father insists on her marriage to the older, more class-appropriate Wolmar, Rousseau's women seem appropriately revealed as mere pawns in a game controlled by men. His work seems to be a classic example of how male society is created and dependent upon the "traffic in women." As Gayle Rubin argues:

> If women are the gifts, then it is men who are the exchange partners. And it is the partners, not the presents, upon whom reciprocal exchange confers its quasi-mystical powers of social linkage. The relations of such a system are such that women are in no position to realize the benefits of their own circulation. As long as the relations specify that men exchange women, it is men who are the beneficiaries of the product of such exchanges—social organization.[28]

As Rubin persuasively argues, social organization as we know it is predicated on such an exchange of women. This kind of social system mandates the creation of gender roles, obligatory heterosexuality, and the constraint of feminine sexual desire. Rousseau's work, as it has been read by feminist scholars, seems to beautifully and perfectly illustrate this version of male domination.

Yet despite the fact that on the face of it Rousseau does intend to ensure social order through trafficking in women, he also scatters throughout his work seductive clues that prompt one to wonder whether Rousseau finds the price of a social order of this kind to be much too high. For the price is his women—women with whom Rousseau clearly sympathizes and whom he takes the time to develop in such a way that we, as readers, are completely dismayed at their demise. I will return to this theme of the demise of Rousseau's women (and what that reveals) in the chapters that follow.

Let us return to the quote from *Emile* above in order to introduce the portrait of Rousseau's women that challenges the idea that they are merely a fantasized reflection of the male self that serves to reinscribe the man's world as he sees it. If it can be argued that Rousseau moves toward a possible recognition of feminine desire, it can be argued that the kernel of a new kind of politics lies therein.

Feminist scholars have been schooled to read Sophie as a woman created to complete the image of Woman that Emile has in his imagination. As such, it is Emile and his tutor who control the entire process: the meeting of the lovers, the seduction of Sophie by Emile, and Sophie's consequent embrace of her domestic role. Yet even from the context of the brief quote from *Emile* cited above, it seems that there is more to this story than that. In Book V, for example, we learn that it is Sophie who desires, who has conjured up a man who will suit her in her imagination. Sophie claims that rather than live "in despair with a man she does not love," she prefers to "die unhappy and free" (E, V: 404). Sophie values her own desire and freedom so highly that she claims "it is better no longer to exist than to exist only to suffer" (E, V: 404). We learn that her mother, having presided over Sophie's education into the arts of becoming a Woman, finds this a shocking position:

> Struck by this singular discourse, her mother found it too bizarre not to suspect some mystery. Sophie was neither affected nor silly. How had this extravagant delicacy been able to take root in her—she who had been taught from her childhood nothing so much as to adjust herself to the people with whom she had to live and to make a virtue of necessity? (E, V: 404).

This "extravagant delicacy" has taken root precisely because Sophie's desire, subjectivity, and intellect are not totally excised from this text. Despite the presentation of Sophie as a demure and passive model of Woman, her imagination seems to exceed the boundaries of her role. Sophie has long dreamed of the perfect man. Her model comes from an intellectual and literary source, Fénelon's *Adventures of Telemachus*.

Rousseau informs us that "Sophie loved Telemachus and loved him with a passion of which nothing could cure her" (E, V: 405). When her parents laughingly suggest that her desire is a "mania," Sophie uses "her own reason" to "reduce them to silence" (E, V: 405).

It is important to note that after having let Sophie's desire momentarily interrupt and disrupt his narrative, Rousseau attempts to foreclose it before it wreaks havoc on his plan for Emile and Sophie to unite in a microcosm of his social order:

> Let us resuscitate this lovable girl to give her a less lively imagination and a happier destiny. I wanted to depict an ordinary woman, and by dint of elevating her soul I have disturbed her reason. I went astray myself (E, V: 405).

Yet though Rousseau devises a plan to get back on track, he continues to wander astray. As we see from the excerpt, it seems that despite the tutor's and Sophie's father's attempt to manipulate the situation and engage in the "exchange of women" to seal the bond between men, it is Sophie who finds her desire fulfilled. When Emile and his tutor arrive at the house of Sophie and her parents, Emile does not realize that Sophie is the woman for him. Ignorant of *Telemachus*, Emile does not even understand the reference to the "charms of Eucharis." Sophie, on the other hand, is in control not only of the literary references, but also of the situation at hand. She feigns a modest air and lowered eyes, but "her tender heart palpitates with joy" at the coming fulfillment of her own desire.

As I will demonstrate from *La Nouvelle Héloïse,* Julie is much bolder than is Sophie in planning and executing the fulfillment of her desire. Again, we are accustomed to reading Julie's story as one wherein she is manipulated by the men in her life. Though this is often the case (after all, she is a woman trying to live within a man's world and within a man's text), we will see that it is *also* true that Julie protests this order in countless ways. Though raised in an aristocratic family, Julie engages in an illicit affair with the petit bourgeois St. Preux. Though virginity and chastity are the supreme virtues for women, Julie knowingly and purposefully makes arrangements to have secret intimate relations with her lover; though she succumbs to her father's will in cutting off her relationship with St. Preux and agrees to marry her father's friend Wolmar, she does so only out of guilt for her mother's death, and she never wholly conquers her desire for her lover. In the quote above from *La Nouvelle Héloïse*, Julie proclaims to St. Preux that despite all odds against them, their "destinies are forever united." She orders her lover to leave their fate in her hands because she knows his heart better than he does and because in her knowledge of love she is better schooled in the art of reason. I will elucidate how Julie makes the connection between compassion and reason and why the novel makes a compelling case for using one's heart to evaluate politics in Chapter 3.

Rousseau's women, rather than his men, demonstrate the empathy and compassion for which Rousseau is famous, and they are able to use these emotional strengths to compel a reasonable political order. In contrast, Rousseau's men are consistently willing to disregard the feelings and lives of others in order to fulfill the destiny, or general will, of the fatherland (interestingly and ironically, a more passionate end). Rousseau's women follow their own desire, bring the lives of marginalized individuals like themselves into focus, and exhibit unparalleled compassion for the suffering of the excluded. We are told by Rousseau that there are moments when this compassion borders on madness. After witnessing the death of her beloved Julie in her arms, Rousseau's Claire is described as

> completely out of her mind, seeing nothing, hearing nothing, recognizing no one, rolling around on the floor wringing her hands and biting the legs of the chairs, murmuring some extravagant words in a muted voice, then at long intervals uttering piercing cries that made one start. (J, VI:XI, 602)

Witnessing this scene, Wolmar is utterly bewildered by the excess of Claire's grief. In comparing himself to Claire, Wolmar notices that his own sorrow is "cold" (J, VI:XI, 606). Looking through men's eyes, women's passion "verges on madness" and appears "laughable" to such "disinterested observers" (J, VI:XI, 606). Wolmar's inability to understand Claire's grief (and women's desire) indicates Rousseau's simultaneous fear and acknowledgment of women's autonomous desire and his subsequent need to block it.

In her evaluation of the French Revolution, Hannah Arendt has raised questions about whether compassion must always remain without words to express it, or whether once expressed it degenerates into a dangerous and devious version of pity. In light of the experience of Rousseau's women, we might add another to the list of Arendt's questions: Why, even when compassion is expressed, does it often fail to be heeded as a critique of instrumental political reason? Though within Rousseau's texts women's words are quite subversive, even radically other, either the women rarely speak or when they do speak, their words go unheeded. Sophie, especially, is known for her demure demeanor; and though Julie is far more outspoken, her words fail to affect a difference. Julie protests her father's insistence that she marry Wolmar and deny her love for St. Preux; she complains to her cousin Claire of Wolmar's lack of affection and cold behavior; and most interesting, within her exchange of letters with Claire, she articulates a compelling critique of the rules that govern Clarens. Despite all that talk, Clarens remains the same. In the end Julie must kill herself in protest of the walls that meet her desire.

Arendt offers the explanation that compassion, or empathy, can only work well on an individual level. We might sympathize with the plight of these characters, but there are no words that would express their plight as a political condition. Arendt remarks that "passion and compassion are not speechless, but their language consists in gestures and expressions of countenance rather than in words."[29] In this interpretation, emotions are too intense; there is a proximity to compassion that makes it unspeakable. And without words, there is no claim to political action that inhabits a political space where we exercise our freedom as speakers of words and doers of deeds:

> Because compassion abolishes the distance, the worldly space between men where political matters, the whole realm of human affairs, are located, it remains, politically speaking, irrelevant and without consequence.[30]

When we do attempt to generalize individual compassion to the political force of pity, the situation becomes even more dangerous. According to Arendt, when this occurs there is a pretense of sensitivity to the suffering of others without an actual knowledge of any person's particular suffering. Moreover, Arendt warns that taking suffering public threatens to eradicate the distinction between private and public, exposing and subverting private emotions when under public scrutiny and conferring power on those who are able to make the marginalized "objects" of pity.

As noted earlier, I will return to Arendt's warnings throughout, especially in Chapter 2 when discussing Sophie's wordless ability to "read" the minds of others, and in Chapter 4 when discussing Staël's attraction to the compassion that Rousseau's women exhibit as a possible ground for an alternative practice of political deliberation. Staël is able to expand fruitfully on Rousseau's conception of empathy as an indicator of a more just politics; she counters Arendt with a feminist argument in critically discussing the exercise of compassion of women in the private sphere as a radical critique of politics as usual in the male forum. When Staël discusses individual women's lives, either fictional (as in the case of Delphine and Corinne) or real (as in the case of Marie-Antoinette), she intends to awaken compassion in a public audience—not by making women objects of pity, but by *instructing* her audience on the outrageous and egregious harms done to women and other marginalized and excluded "others." The women in Staël's work are remarkably able to bring injustice to light. Staël's women do find words to speak; they speak loudly and critically of the politics that excludes them.

The excerpt above from Staël's *Delphine* is, in fact, about a woman speaking. When Delphine meets Léonce, a man to whom she is attracted despite their differences, she attracts his attention through speaking with him (and as Staël elaborates, also "in front of him" and "for him") about intellectual and literary matters. Delphine is no demure woman; as we will learn, she is known for her outspoken opinions on revolution, on freedom, on divorce, and on the general state of affairs in France (the novel is set during the early stages of the Revolution to the deposition of the king). She proclaims those opinions in the many salons of Paris. In portraying the character of Delphine, Staël illustrates the role of women in the formation and critique of Enlightenment ideals.

Against the interpretation of Enlightenment salons as places where women sought power through their relationship with men, Dena Goodman argues that by establishing a space for, and engaging in, serious conversation, women played an invaluable role in forging an alternative community (to the Old Regime) based in "values of reciprocity and exchange."[31] In speaking of Germaine de Staël's mother, Suzanne Necker, Goodman writes:

> The attention Necker paid to the written and spoken word, and to books and people through them, was also the principle by which she conducted her salon and which she strove to instill in others. Thus a conversation was effective when everyone's attention was fixed; a good reading fixed the attention of the listeners. "This precept of permanent attention to a single object," she wrote, "is applicable to business, to study, and to conversation."[32]

From her mother, Staël clearly learned to value intellectual conversation; she instills this in the heroines of her novels to create strong women skilled in the art of speaking and paying attention. In the passage above taken from *Corinne, or Italy*, we see Corinne through the eyes of her future lover, Oswald. In this scene, Corinne is being crowned as a goddess of Italy renowned for her skill in the realms of poetry and conversation. Corinne's talents with words are so impressive as to dub her *improvisatrice:* an artist known to improvise verse on any given subject. Indeed, Corinne is *empowered* through her own words: Staël writes that when Corinne speaks, she is transformed from a "fearful woman" into an "inspired priestess, joyously devoting herself to the cult of genius;" her enthusiasm and self-confidence stem directly from having "just spoken, filling her soul with the noblest thoughts."

Not surprisingly, these powerfully speaking women that Staël creates know how to express and act on their desire. Delphine and Corinne each initiate their respective relationships with men. As in the quotes from Rousseau at the beginning of this section, the passages from Staël's novels indicate that it is the women who, in these situations, are in control. Léonce does not speak, but merely listens to Delphine's words; Oswald comes forward to speak to Corinne, but is unable to "master the embarrassment holding him back." Each woman also, through actions and words, specifies a detailed critique of the present social/political situation and articulates an alternative based in a feminine sensibility. In the chapters on Staël, I will pursue Staël's criticisms of the manly citizen and the masculinist public sphere. I will argue that Staël draws on the feminine in Rousseau in terms of both critique and vision, but manages to take us much farther than we could go with Rousseau's Sophie or Julie.

There are at least two kinds of criticisms that can be made of Staël's idea of the strong woman and, as I will elaborate, the qualities of the woman as citizen. One is that she merely substitutes female power for male power, with the feminine alternative drawing perilously close to the male version of Woman. Staël does indeed speak of women's compassion, women's art of loving, the knowledge women have in their hearts—all of which raise red flags for feminists accustomed to hearing these kinds of arguments made by men in order to limit women's participation in the public world of politics. In Staël's defense of Marie-Antoinette at the time of her trial and execution, for example, Staël argues that the queen could not have committed the terrible crimes of which she was accused because she had a "woman's heart" and knew how to love (Q, 372). In her defense of the queen, Staël asks women to respond to her plight based on a recognition of their own similarity to Marie-Antoinette *as women*. See how Marie-Antoinette *is just like you— your destiny could be hers*, she argues: "if you are sensitive, if you are mothers, she has loved with all of the same power of soul as you" (Q, 373). Here we clearly see that in Staël's account of women's compassion, the bonds of women's friendship, and the use of love and pity as alternative political principles, Staël can be read as positing a mere substitution of Woman for masculine principles.

In a seemingly odd counter-reading of Staël, she is not read as substituting Woman's morality for male power politics, but as simply desiring that women be granted a piece of the male pie. In these readings, Staël is advanced as the theorist of the "exceptional woman."[33] Most often in readings that coin Staël in this manner, Staël's heroines are seen to be reflections of Staël herself (or as women engaged in various scenarios that play out how Staël would have liked to have been recognized). As superior women able to beat the odds, they successfully challenge conventions and have their voices recognized by powerful men. In this interpretation, to be an "exceptional woman" is to deny the condition of all other women; it is most literally to speak, exceptionally, *unlike* a woman and *like* a man.

My interpretation will acknowledge the basis of both of these kinds of readings of Staël's work and note that both are borne out in certain passages and texts. My reading does not, however, leave Staël as hopelessly confused about whether she is a feminist and if so, of what particular persuasion. Whether she was a feminist, and if so, what that might mean, was obviously not one of Staël's pressing concerns. This does not mean that we cannot, or should not, ask these questions of Staël's work. In fact, in exploring her texts for a possible recognition of feminine difference, I ask precisely these kinds of questions of her and of her work. But it is important to note that they are *my* concerns and not Staël's.

Though readings of Staël as "difference" feminist and "equality on male terms" feminist are both possible, to understand Staël's project the two kinds of readings must be considered together in their historical context. Staël wrote at a pivotal moment when the "universal" rights of equality were being denied to women on the basis of their "difference." Staël herself desperately desired to be included in the "male" political process but was denied access solely on account of her sex. She quickly noticed that to be a woman during the revolutionary process was to be part of an increasingly political and manipulated category. One of the strengths of Staël's critique of masculine power and potential feminine subversion comes from her insight that within the revolutionary social/political situation, women's political strategies stemmed from the effacement of all but two options: equality on male terms (either as the liberal or republican model) or the critique of male terms through an emphasis on women's deviation from those norms. As an unflinching political activist for women's rights, Staël was willing to try either or both of these strategies at what she deemed as the appropriate moments. Hence, for example, her defense of Marie-Antoinette as demure and loving mother (the idealization of Woman) at the time when she was being vilified in the press as the manipulator of the king, a power-hungry priestess, a man disguised as a woman.[34]

Ultimately, however, neither strategy was successful in achieving an equality for women that would not devalue the feminine. Yet because of the historical moment when Staël wrote, and because she was so taken with the feminine presence in Rousseau, I find her a fascinating figure to whom I can pose the questions that I find most compelling for twentieth-century feminist theory. When Staël's work is read in its entirety, the hint of a third way, a third possible strategy, emerges. In associating the feminine with face-to-face relations, a concern for individual lives, the value of emotional and familial ties, and a focus on the particular as opposed to the universal, Staël points toward a model for citizenship that transforms democratic practice. This model emerges from Staël's work amidst the many political strategies she advances and the conflicting arguments she employs. I will argue that the notion of the feminine and the recognition of sexual difference more generally is not merely the flip side of male power as the idea of Woman. Intertwining Rousseau's and Staël's insights, I will claim that the location of the subversive feminine within the manly citizen fully disrupts the idea of positing any true or essential identity. It follows that no identity, including a feminine identity, is a fixed essence. The feminine points elsewhere; I hope to map that direction.

Within this text I specify how the feminine presence in Rousseau and Staël functions as a site of subversion that disrupts (as it constitutes) the manly citizen and masculine politics. This feminine presence not only manages as a critique but also as a vision toward an alternative. A recognition of sexual difference (rather than the elimination of sexual difference) is necessary to begin to effect this alternative. I argue that politics and citizenship would look very different in such a polity, taking us beyond the impasse between liberals and communitarians as well as debates between equality and difference in feminist theory. I will seek to fulfill the promise of these arguments throughout the text.

Affirming Feminine Difference

> The girl indeed, has nothing more to fear since she has *nothing* to lose. Since she has no representation of what she might fear to lose. Since what she might, potentially, lose, has no value.
>
> —LUCE IRIGARAY, *Speculum of the Other Woman*

I quote Irigaray's critique of Freud in order to emphasize what is potentially so subversive about feminine difference when it is recognized.

Irigaray maintains that Freud's contribution to masculinist psychoanalytic theory is his way of seeing the little girl solely in terms of the little boy. Freud maintains that when the girl recognizes her lack of the little boy's penis, she will "strive to become him, to mimic him, to seduce him in order to get one."[35] Here Woman is conceived only in terms of her lack of what man has. Within this order, which Irigaray maintains is typical of Western psychoanalysis and metaphysics, Woman can be articulated only as either not-man or other-than-man. Women are subsumed, then, within categories that measure them in terms of a lack of maleness or a mirror opposite reflection of maleness.

In the quote above, Irigaray maintains that the girl has nothing to lose in this symbolic order because she is never represented within this order. In other words, within the masculine symbolic, there is no place for the feminine. What we know of feminine has only been what man has posited as Woman. We have not been able to discover true feminine, or sexual, difference within the "economy of the same." To discover and recognize the feminine would entail a radical disruption of philosophy and politics as we know it. As articulated in *This Sex Which Is Not One*,[36] Irigaray locates the potential of that discovery of feminine difference in women's bodies, in women's erotic desire, in the many ways that women fail to conform to the male reduction of the many to the one, the particular to the general, poetry to philosophy.

Though I too will argue the importance and political potential of recognizing feminine difference, my text parts ways with Irigaray's analysis in my claim, articulated in my reading of Rousseau, that the masculine identity is never fully realized by the displacement, forgetting, or exclusion of the feminine. In my examination of the manly citizen as found in Rousseau, I will argue that the feminine can never completely be forgotten. The feminine is always lurking around the corner, as it were, or even more boldly at the intersection, of the economy of the same. This feminine presence is radically disruptive of any claim to constitute male identity, displace otherness, and posit a citizenship based on the "general" will.

The feminine difference at the heart of the manly citizen is waiting to be discovered. This is what I will try to do in pasting together the gestures and words of Rousseau's and Staël's women, which reach toward an alternative space for politics and alternative ways of conceptualizing identity and citizenship. This effort can never be complete in the sense that it would go against the impulse of my project to articulate a version of citizenship that is fixed, true, and unchanging. Nevertheless, I will take the risk of gesturing in the direction of a politics unwilling to efface difference, eliminate particularity, and deny alterity.

2

(Re)examining the Feminine Presence

Rousseau's Sophie

•

Rousseau feared that, given the chance to speak in public, women would undermine his plan for the good society. Not only must public spaces therefore be secured from the feminine presence, but in addition, almost all casual commerce between men and women must be restricted. Rousseau is famous for his proposal to mandate an education whereby men and women are taught to assume their gendered roles "instinctively." At the behest of this education men become manly citizens while women take on the characteristics of Woman, a private creature who is the idealized essence of man's desire. This arrangement makes it possible for public spaces to be reserved for men while Woman stays at home. The feminine presence must be safely displaced, indeed forgotten, in order for men to become the manly citizens.

Such an extreme position directs my attention to the women Rousseau describes in his work. If Rousseau's women are safely ensconced at home, why does it remain so difficult for his men to forget the feminine? It is almost as if neither male public space *nor* men's confidence in their masculinity are ever totally secure from the threat of encroachment by women. What is so dangerous about what women might say? What is it about women's education, women's ways of knowing, the things women like to do, the ways in which women communicate with others that makes the feminine such an immanent threat?

In the chapters on Rousseau's *Emile* and *La Nouvelle Héloïse* that follow, I will map Rousseau's attempt to constitute identity in terms of the manly citizen. Rousseau's manly citizen is taught to realize his identity as manifest in the projection of the free will of each as the general will of all. But from the perspective of Rousseau's women, a vantage point to which I am attracted by Rousseau's own sympathetic portrayal of these women, attempts to construct manly citizenship and forge a unanimous general will result in a complete and utter failure of identity. Mapping Rousseau's failure sheds light on the source of his difficulty: the feminine presence as constant disruption, as continual reminder of the inability to efface difference and to project each as a coherent and stable self. Focus on this subversive feminine presence points the way toward recognition of an alternative democratic principle at the heart of Rousseau's work.

The Fragile Construction of Gender in Rousseau's Community

In the *Government of Poland*, Rousseau argues that "among the ancients" he finds three legislators "so outstanding as to deserve our special mention: Moses, Lycurgus, and Numa" (GP, 5). What made each of these ancient legislators great was that they were able to take individual men—whether a "swarm of wretched fugitives," a people "debased by servitude" and "vices," or a "band of robbers"—instill in them a "burning love of country," and create a "political society, a free people" (GP, 6–7). The secret to the success of the ancients is that they made individual men into *brothers* in the service of the *fatherland*. Each man, as citizen, was willing to relinquish his individual freedom for the good of all in the general will. Rousseau argues that the social compact can be expressed in the following terms:

> *Each of us puts his person and all his power in common under the supreme direction of the general will, and, in our corporate capacity, we receive each member as an indivisible part of the whole* (SC, 192).

This plan works by the exchange of one kind of freedom for another. In becoming a citizen, each man must be willing and able to sacrifice his freedom as an individual in order to think as his best self in determining, and subsequently living by, what is good for the whole society. Rousseau puts it this way:

> In fact, each individual, as a man, may have a particular will contrary or dissimilar to the general will that he has as a citizen. His particular inter-

est may speak to him quite differently from the common interest . . . [to assert this particular will] could not but prove the undoing of the body politic. . . . This means nothing less than that he will be forced to be free; for this is the condition which, by giving each citizen to his country, secures him against all personal dependence (SC, 194–195).

In the place of the liberal individual self as freewheeling, autonomous, egocentric, and radically disconnected from others, Rousseau advances the idea of the citizen. Tracy Strong has argued that for Rousseau, being a citizen is rooted in the ability to recognize what is "common" to all humans within one's own self as the possessor of a free will.[1] This free will makes it possible for all to act in concert rather than as isolated individuals each vying for power and self-interest. This construction of the citizen as against the individual cuts against liberal autonomy. Here, free will is understood as the outgrowth of what is common and good for all of us as a society (and hence, the "general" will). Indeed, individuals achieve a stable identity (if this is possible) only as part and parcel of the general will.

Penny Weiss points out that "Rousseau shares with many feminists a condemnation of central features of liberalism and an endorsement of community".[2] Yet as Weiss also notes, communitarian thinkers have often been hostile toward feminism. This hostility toward feminism (marked as a hostility toward women's desire and all it represents) stems, in part, from the "logic of identity" that undergirds the quest for community as well as the quest for liberal individualism. As Iris Marion Young explains:

> Each entails a denial of difference and a desire to bring multiplicity and heterogeneity into unity, though in opposing ways. Liberal individualism denies difference by positing the self as a solid, self-sufficient unity, not defined by anything or anyone other than itself. Its formalistic ethic of rights also denies difference by bringing all such separated individuals under a common measure of rights. Proponents of community, on the other hand, deny difference by positing fusion rather than separation as the social ideal. They conceive the social subject as a relation of unity or mutuality composed by identification and symmetry among individuals within a totality. Communitarianism represents an urge to see persons in unity with one another in a shared whole.[3]

As an exemplary form of republican community, Rousseau's general will has been praised by communitarians and criticized by feminists.[4] Regardless of political perspective, however, all interpreters of Rousseau agree on this central element of his thought: under the guidelines of Rousseau's social contract, women are not able to become citizens. To be a citizen of Rousseau's republic, one must first be a man. In her compelling analysis of the specifics of Rousseau's sexual contract, Linda M. G. Zerilli argues:

> Rousseau's repeated and familiar warnings against the "disorder of women" evince his fear that, if the code of gender difference is not strictly adhered to at each and every moment, all is lost. There will not be any citizens because there will not be any men. . . . To represent themselves as members of the republic, men must first contract to represent themselves as members of their own sex.[5]

For men to "contract to represent themselves as members of their own sex" is the linchpin of the good society. The stable and coherent identity of *men as men* is at the core of society maintaining its identity as the *fatherland*. Here the will of each individual man is fulfilled in the general will; each man locates his own identity as a man and citizen within the myths of the fatherland. The myth of the male fatherland as the central organizing tenet of manly citizenship is made quite clear in Rousseau's recommendations to the government of Poland. Rousseau's novel ideas about how such a mythic identity rooted in loyalty could possibly be instilled in such a motley group of humans are worth quoting at length:

> I recommend numerous public games, where Poland, like a good mother, can take delight in seeing her children at play. Let Poland's mind be on them often, so that their minds will always be on Poland. You should prohibit—even, because of the example, at court—the amusements that one ordinarily finds in courts: gambling, the theater, comedies, operas—everything that makes men unmanly, or distracts them, or isolates them, or causes them to forget their fatherland and their duties, or disposes them to feel content anywhere so long as they are being amused (GP, 14).

It is important to recognize a central theme in the connection between the fatherland, manliness, and the general will: all are threatened by women and by the encroachment of the feminine. In his *Letter to M. D'Alembert on the Theatre*, Rousseau vehemently opposes the introduction of a theatre to Geneva because it would corrupt good citizens. He argues that when people are *already* corrupted, the theatre might be good for them: for "distracting people from their miseries;" "perfecting taste when dignity is gone;" "preventing bad morals from degenerating into brigandage" (LD'A, 64). This is not, however, the case in Geneva. Here the citizens are good: they are devoted to public duty; they remain untouched by the vices of a big city such as Paris. Thus, the introduction of the theatre in Geneva would serve

> to destroy the love of work; to discourage industry; to ruin individuals; to inspire them with the taste for idleness; to make them seek for the means of subsistence without doing anything; to render a people inactive and slack; to prevent it from seeing the public and private goals with which it ought to busy itself; to turn prudence to ridicule; to substitute a theatrical jargon for the practice of the virtues; to make metaphysic of all morality; to turn citizens into wits, housewives into bluestockings, and daughters into sweethearts out of the drama. (LD'A, 64)

The theatre is such a corrupting influence because of the pride of place it gives to love, the "realm of women" (LD'A, 47). When the love interest is so strongly emphasized and reinforced in the theatre, women are given prominence. The portrayal of the ways, manners, and customs of women as seen on stage (particularly as concerning matters of love) undermines men's ability to distinguish themselves from women. As Rousseau puts it:

> [T]his weaker sex, not in the position to take on our way of life, which is too hard for it, forces us to take on its way, too soft for us; and, no longer wishing to tolerate separation, unable to make themselves into men, *the women make us into women*. This disadvantageous result which degrades man is very important everywhere; but it is especially so in states like ours, whose interest it is to prevent it. Whether a monarch governs men or women ought to be rather indifferent to him, provided that he be obeyed; but in a republic, men are needed. (LD'A, 100, my emphasis)

Yes, men are needed—but where to find them? Masculinity, as constructed and promoted by Rousseau, is extremely fragile. One of Rousseau's most strident criticisms of monarchy is that under a monarchy, gender boundaries collapse. Rousseau disdainfully observes that in Paris "every woman . . . gathers in her apartment a harem of men more womanish than she" (LD'A, 100). Even the casual presence of women threatens the integrity of masculinity. "Never has a people perished from an excess of wine; all perish from the disorder of women" (LD'A, 109).

Elizabeth Wingrove notes that "republican identity itself originates with the control of sexual performance."[6] Gender identity (teaching men to be men and women to be idealized versions of Woman) is *the* necessary fiction at the heart of Rousseau's politics. To *become a gender*, whether man or Woman, is absolutely necessary for Rousseau's political and social contract to function properly; yet no one must speak openly of the performative aspects involved. Frightened by the possibility that gender boundaries do not exist naturally, Rousseau seizes on the idea that gender boundaries are absolutely essential to a good society. *The Second Discourse* confirms Rousseau's belief that we are naturally isolated and autonomous beings in the state of nature. As a device to move us from there (the state of nature) to where he desires that we go (the good society based in the social contract), Rousseau creates gender roles that will ensure our interdependence. Penny Weiss wisely reminds us that Rousseau does not think that the sexes are relevantly differentiated by nature; rather, "sex differences can and should be created, encouraged, and enforced because of their social consequences, which he considers to be both necessary and beneficial."[7]

With gender carefully and meticulously constructed by Rousseau, the republican way of life sets a rigid standard for sex differentiation. In order to secure his republic from the threat of feminine disruption, Rousseau proposes that the *cercles* provide the main mode of social gathering. These are separate spheres whereby men and women teach themselves the virtue of performing their respective genders. As Rousseau puts it:

> Let us follow the indications of nature, let us consult the good of society; we shall find that the two sexes ought to come together sometimes and to live separated ordinarily. I said it before concerning women, I say it now concerning men. They are affected as much as, and more than,

women by a commerce that is too intimate; they lose not only their morals, but we lose our morals and our constitution. (LD'A, 100)

All these efforts are meant as measures to promote the stable identity of the manly citizen. As part of this project, Rousseau seems to clearly specify the way women are to act. Women's education is channeled in particular ways to create Woman, a seemingly less threatening version of the feminine presence.

Feminist Readings of Sophie

Feminist readings of Rousseau have taken their cue from Rousseau's in-famous description of Sophie in Book V of *Emile:*

Sophie ought to be a woman as Emile is a man—that is to say, she ought to have everything which suits the constitution of her species and her sex in order to fill her place in the physical and moral order. (E, V:357)

Feminists have rightly criticized the misogynist Rousseau, who defines Woman as he might like her to be, a mirror opposite of the male image. Susan Okin remarks that Rousseau was "not at all interested in discovering what women's natural potential might enable her to achieve, but was simply concerned with suiting her to her role as man's subordinate complement in the patriarchal family."[8]

Choosing certain passages that describe Sophie as Emile's perfect mate, Sophie has been typically read as a mouthpiece of masculine desire. One of the first analyses and condemnations of Rousseau's description of Woman appears in Mary Wollstonecraft's 1792 *Vindication of the Rights of Woman.* Wollstonecraft singles out Rousseau's description of young girls in which he cites their natural inclination toward adornment, being pretty, and being thought pretty:

Observe a little girl spending the day around her doll, constantly changing its clothes, dressing and undressing it hundreds and hundreds of times, continuously seeking new combinations of ornaments—well- or ill-matched, it makes no difference. Her fingers lack adroitness, her taste is not yet formed, but already the inclination reveals itself. In this eternal occupation time flows without her thinking of it; the hours pass, and she knows nothing of it. She even forgets meals. She is hungrier for adornment than for food. . . . In fact, almost all little girls learn to read and write with repugnance. But as for holding a needle, that they always learn gladly. They imagine themselves to be grown up and think with pleasure that these talents will one day be useful for adorning themselves. (E, V:367–368)

Rousseau is attempting to argue here that differences between the sexes are based in nature. Clearly it is a weak attempt; Rousseau did not consider either nature or science to be judicious and reliable determinants for gender difference. At times he readily infers that sexual difference is merely a product of social expediency: women must be seen as chaste to preserve the reputation of their husbands; fathers must think that their children are their own; men and women must each be incomplete in order to become interdependent. Certain women might claim that women's ways are a direct reflection of the education they have been given by men; Rousseau asserts that it is women *themselves* who teach young girls the art of performing their femininity:

> Is it our [men's] fault that they [women] please us when they are pretty, that their mincing ways seduce us, that the art which they learn from you attracts us and pleases us, that we like to see them tastefully dressed, that we let them sharpen at their leisure the weapons with which they subjugate us? (E, V:363)

Wollstonecraft responds that indeed it is, that because Rousseau had his own unruly passions, he placed them onto women in order to justify men's use of women, both sexually and politically. According to Wollstonecraft:

> [Rousseau's] imagination constantly prepared inflammable fuel for his inflammable senses; but, in order to reconcile his respect for self-denial, fortitude, and those heroic virtues, which a mind like his could not coolly admire, he labours to invert the law of nature, and broaches a doctrine pregnant with mischief and derogatory to the character of supreme wisdom.[9]

Wollstonecraft reflects that Rousseau has not only got it all wrong, but he's got it wrong precisely because his personal desires dictate his "philosophical" reflection: he remarks that women are a certain way (sexually promiscuous and powerful over men and the family) only in order to legitimately deny women any public power and any access to man's world. On this account, Rousseau's remarks on the nature of women are simply a mirror image of his own desires for and about women. This criticism is repeated in Jean Bethke Elshtain's analysis of Rousseau:

> Rousseau believed that women already possessed power on so many levels vis-à-vis men and children, simply by virtue of their being what they were, that they neither "needed" nor could be trusted with power of a public, political sort. Women were volatile and must be reined in, forced to be content to wield their power "privately."[10]

As is clear from Elshtain's comments, Wollstonecraft's early writings on Rousseau's description of femininity have informed subsequent feminist critiques. Rousseau's depiction of the feminine, particularly as embodied in Sophie, his ideal woman, has been deemed a caricature of Woman, a truncated version of anything a woman might desire or achieve.[11] Sophie desires only to be a helpmate to Emile; As Rousseau himself puts it:

> Thus the whole education of women ought to relate to men. To please men, to be useful to them, to make herself loved and honored by them, to raise them when young, to care for them when grown, to counsel them, to console them, to make their lives agreeable and sweet—these are the duties of women at all times. (E, V: 365)

Confirmation of this interpretation of Rousseau whereby the feminine is solely determined by male desire is readily available throughout Rousseau's oeuvre. Countless passages describe women as meek, unquestioning, quick to please men, and desiring solely to admire and serve their husbands/lovers. Rousseau's two well-known descriptions of woman's nature, the dangerous coquette and the subjugated wife, are seemingly complementary versions of male desire. Men easily master both kinds of women: if masculinity itself has a secure basis, femininity is merely its opposite, able to be manipulated and controlled at man's behest. Yet if this were the only version of the feminine represented in Rousseau, why would men need to be fearful?

Another Look at Sophie

Since gender is learned, it is never complete. "Man," "woman," and "citizen" are each fragile constructions in Rousseau's oeuvre. Identity is never as stable as Rousseau desires. The feminine is never quite as contained as he would like it to be. Sustained analysis of the feminine in Rousseau produces a surprising result: Rousseau's women really are subversive of the kind of polity Rousseau seeks to create. Moreover, Rousseau is ever aware of, constantly flirting with, this danger. What is, after all, so dangerous about Sophie? In which ways does she exceed man's imagination, his controllable other? What might her actions reveal about a democratic alternative in Rousseau's politics?

Sophie is educated to be the ideal woman for Emile. Her nature is "good;" she has a "very sensitive heart;" her face is "ordinary but agreeable;" her "expression gives promise of a soul and does not lie; one can approach her with indifference but not leave her without emotion" (E, V:393). As Rousseau describes her, it is the combination of qualities in Sophie that makes her character so appealing; moreover, she even knows how to turn her defects into virtues. For instance, though Sophie has no talent for music and cannot read a note, she has a taste for music that makes her remarkably able to feel the "charms of expression" and "love music for itself" (E, V:394). Though she is a glutton by nature, loving all sweets and tending to eat them excessively, Sophie has learned that sugar spoils her teeth and fattens her figure. Guided by virtue, she eats only very moderate amounts of everything (E, V:395). Though gaiety and spontaneity come naturally to Sophie, if she is seen enjoying herself too readily, she breaks out in a modest blush (E, V:396). When her feelings are hurt, which they often are due to her sensitive heart, Sophie does not pout, but her heart swells. She rushes to get away to cry so as not to burden others with her sadness (E, V:396).

Sophie's knowledge does not derive from books or from intellectual rigor. Her mind has been formed through interactions with others, attention to detail, conversations with her mother and father, her own reflections, and the observations she has made in "the little bit of the world she has seen" (E, V:396).

Sophie is not entirely exempt from caprice, but when she falters, her shame stems from the knowledge of the offense she has committed, rather than the punishment exacted (E, V:396). Even if nothing is said to her, she will hasten to make amends for her offense in an attempt to recover her virtue. The "need to love" devours Sophie (E, V:397). Most important, she treats others with respect and commitment. "She would kiss the ground before the lowliest domestic without this abasement causing her the least discomfort . . . in a word, she suffers the wrongs of others with patience and makes amends for their own with pleasure" (E, V:396). So far, this is hardly the description of a dangerous woman. Yet, when we compare ideal woman to ideal man, Sophie to Emile, we begin to see the ways in which Sophie's art of interaction directly challenges Emile's view of the world.

In her education as a Woman, Sophie has been taught to watch for subtle gestures that indicate how other people perceive any given situation. She lives outside herself for the most part, sensitive to the hurt feelings or exclusion (perceived or real) of those unlike herself. Emile, in contrast, has been taught to isolate his own experience and place it onto others as the common experience of all. Consider, for example, Rousseau's description of the different ways a man and a woman behave at a dinner party:

> I go to parties at which master and mistress jointly do the honors. . . . The husband omits no care in order to be attentive to all. He goes; he comes; he makes his rounds and puts himself out in countless ways; he would like to be all attentiveness. . . . [As for the woman] . . . nothing takes place that she does not notice; no one leaves to whom she has not spoken; she has omitted nothing that could interest everyone; she has said nothing to anyone that was not agreeable to him; and without in any way upsetting the order, the least important person among her company is no more forgotten than the most important. . . . Dinner is served. All go to the table. The man, knowledgeable about who gets along with whom, will seat them on the basis of what he knows. The woman, without knowing anything, will make no mistakes about it. She will have already read in their eyes and in their bearing, everything about who belongs with whom, and each guest will find himself placed where he wants to be. I do not say that when the food is served, no one is forgotten. But even though the master of the house may have forgotten no one when he passed around the food, his wife goes further and divines what you look at with pleasure and offers you some. In speaking to her neighbor, she has her eye on the end of the table; she distinguishes between the guest who does not eat because he is not hungry, and the one who does not dare to help himself or to ask because he is awkward or

timid. On leaving the table each guest believes that she has thought only of him (E, V:383–384).

This excerpt illustrates Rousseau's model of man's and woman's gendered roles in community. Able to see what is common in all based on what he knows of himself, the man "omits no care to be attentive to all" and seats persons in a satisfactory way. In other words, the man is fair, impartial, and knowledgeable; and he applies a universal standard (again, based in what he knows of himself) to all at the party. He tries to speak to each and for the same amount of time, but some might be forgotten in the process. The woman, on the other hand, makes certain that "the least important person among her company is no more forgotten than the most important." She is attentive to the slightest gesture. She can distinguish between the one who does not eat because she is not hungry and the one who does not eat because she is too shy to ask for food. Because man is looking to see what is common in all, he cannot see, cannot hear, those who are different or those who have life experiences that require them to express themselves in ways unfamiliar to him. In contrast, the woman, who has made a "profound study of the mind of man—not an abstraction of the mind of man in general, but the minds of the men around her" (E, V:387)—is able to decipher the languages of those who speak differently. The woman has honed observing and listening to an art. She "has seen what was whispered at the other end of the room; she knows what this person thought, to what this remark or that gesture related" (E, V:384).

From this description of the dinner party, we can extract what looks to be two different models for citizenship. As I have already indicated, the model based on Emile's behavior is one in which the community will, or the general will, is located by the male citizen who looks deep inside himself; he seeks to find what is common to all within himself and then to apply this uniformly to everyone at the party. I contend that this model forces everyone to speak in the same language in order to be heard. Some commentators have said otherwise. For example, in an analysis of the "politics of the ordinary" in Rousseau, Tracy Strong has remarked that Rousseau is *not* a theorist of the unified self—human beings are, rather, composite in Rousseau's mind.[12] "Our commonalty—

the stuff of humanity—requires difference and there is no identity that is not that of difference."[13] Strong paints a portrait of Rousseau as sensitive to diversity, advancing a model of political space as the location for living with inequality in a way that allows all to remain free. But what of the political context, here the sexual politics, that structures what counts as common, what counts as community, how persons negotiate their relationship to that political space? It remains the case that Rousseau solely advances *man*, not woman, as citizen, and that man is taught certain characteristics (denying or suppressing other characteristics) that make him (through a very particular and controlled education) the best kind of citizen. From Rousseau's description of the dinner party, the man is the one who in knowing himself, *assumes* that he knows others: he is fair, he is impartial, he treats each equally. In seeking the common in himself and in all, Rousseau's man is able to tap into our feelings of human solidarity, of being ourselves with others in a community. Yet this same man cannot detect the voices/gestures of those actually unlike himself. Hannah Arendt also accuses Rousseau of looking only within himself to read the needs of others:

> While the plight of others aroused his heart, he became involved in *his* heart rather than in the sufferings of others, and he was enchanted with its moods and caprices as they disclosed themselves in the sweet delight of intimacy which Rousseau was one of the first to discover and which from then on began playing its important role in the formation of modern sensibility.[14]

Deepening our sense of commonality and community in this particular case requires that all be alike in order to participate in conversation.

And what of the woman in this description? She knows nothing, but is able to read the subtle gestures of each. She is attuned to discord and seeks out those who, for whatever reason, are *in* but not *of* the dinner party. From what we are told, it almost seems as if the woman can read the minds of each of the guests. She "divines what you look at with pleasure and offers you some;" each guest leaves the table believing that "she has thought only of him." Were we to use the woman as a model for citizenship, we would be edging dangerously close to advocating what Iris Marion Young has called the "Rousseauist dream of transparency." This dream is one in which democratic space is structured so that we can privilege face to face relations and see in other persons exactly what they desire; we can communicate immediately and transparently. In speaking of theorists of community who advocate these relations, Young argues:

> Immediacy is better than mediation because immediate relations have the purity and security longed for in the Rousseauist dream: we are transparent to one another, purely copresent in the same time and space, close enough to touch, and nothing comes between us to obstruct our vision of one another.[15]

Young goes on to point out that this ideal is a metaphysical illusion. Even more damning, though, is the notion that this ideal, if advanced by the woman in the dinner party description, could possibly be merely the flip side of the male ideal. While the man arrogantly projects himself onto others, the woman just as arrogantly assumes that she can empathize to such an extent as to read the longings of others. If we read the models in this way, it seems that both ultimately erase others and deny alterity.

If the woman in this passage can be read as merely offering a model that is a mirror opposite of the male, we have not come any distance toward an alternative. Were this the case, we would remain trapped within the logic of identity, the metaphysics of presence, the myth of the stable self. Though the woman described in this passage flirts with the myth of the immediate present and unmediated communication, when read in the context of Rousseau's awe and fear of the feminine, her behavior points elsewhere. As Rousseau mentions, the woman at the dinner party does not know the mind of man in general, but only the minds of those around her. In this sense, it may be that she would be willing to confront the other, whether outside or within herself. Recall also that the woman lives outside of herself. She looks around to others to understand herself and the situation. Emile can only look inside himself; he can only see those who conform to the vision of his own desire. Sophie disrupts his thought in a violent way.

From the very inception of his education, Emile was taught that "a truly happy being is a solitary being" (E, IV: 221). When he reaches adolescence, Emile has no emotional attachment to any other living being aside from his tutor, Jean-Jacques. Only the onset of puberty arouses his passions, threatening the development of *amour-propre*, for "to be loved, one has to make oneself lovable" (E, IV:214). At this critical stage, Jean-Jacques manipulates Emile's potentially dangerous sexuality by attempting to incorporate an ideal of beauty and spirituality into Emile's vision of an object of love. Emile will long for a beautiful, spiritual, virtuous woman to satisfy his sexual desire, binding his lust with the need for true love. If Emile were in the state of nature, any and every woman would be equally able to fulfill his sexual desires (E, II:78). In submitting to sexual desire, interpreted as a direct need for another human being, a possibility is created for both tyranny and slavery—conditions he finds definitive in intimate relationships of mutual dependency. Rousseau wants to bypass both options by making the conditions of autonomy available to Emile.

Emile learns to love, not through an attachment to a real human being, an object outside of himself, but rather by loving an internal image, one supplied to him by his tutor. At Rousseau's insistence, Emile learns the value of autonomy through learning to love an object. In order for Emile's integrity as man and citizen to remain intact, Sophie can only be a "holy image," one to which Emile must initially submit in order to develop the authentic autonomy that is absolutely essential to Rousseau's masculine version of citizenship. When Emile's growing attachment to the flesh and blood Sophie threatens to destroy his autonomy, he must retreat. In the following vignette, Rousseau makes it clear that one cannot be happy if one is dependent on another human being:

> One morning, when they have not seen each other for two days, I enter Emile's room with a letter in my hand; staring fixedly at him, I say, "What would you do if you were informed that Sophie is dead?" He lets out a great cry, gets up, striking his hands together, and looks wild-eyed at me without saying a single word. (E, V: 442)

Emile's response to this false information initiates a conversation in which Emile is warned that his passion for Sophie has threatened all his education meant to achieve, mainly his independence and his preparation for citizenship:

How pitiable you are going to be, thus subjected to your unruly passions! There will always be privations, losses and alarms. . . . The fear of losing everything will prevent you from possessing anything. . . . How will you know how to sacrifice inclination to duty and to hold out against your heart in order to listen to your reason? . . . Learn to become your own master. Command your heart, Emile, and you will be virtuous. (E, V: 444–5)

To remedy his too intense commitment to the woman he loves, Emile is forced to delay his marriage in order to travel through Europe. His trip teaches him to endure life without Sophie. Emile learns his lesson well, carefully guarding his independence and autonomy. He learns to confirm what he knows of himself and deny all that challenges that identity. In order to guard against a confrontation with difference, Emile practices the art of embracing in others only what is the same as what he knows within himself:

He loves men because they are his fellows, but he will especially love those who resemble him most because he will feel that he is good; and since he judges this resemblance by agreement in moral taste, he will be quite gratified to be approved in everything connected with good character. (E, IV:339)

Good character consists of looking deep inside the masculine self to project what he finds there onto all of humanity. When Emile is confronted with Sophie's difference (the feminine subversive), this picture of the world falters. For example, during Emile's and Sophie's courtship, Emile and his tutor come to visit Sophie and her parents almost every day. One day they fail to come. Their absence sends Sophie into a state of extreme anxiety and worry. Later, to explain their negligence, Jean-Jacques tells the story of a gallant Emile who saved an injured man and assisted a woman in labor. Emile turns to Sophie to say:

Sophie, you are the arbiter of my fate. You know it well. You can make me die of pain. But do not hope to make me forget the rights of humanity. They are more sacred to me than yours. I will never give them up for you. (E, V: 441)

Though deeply in love with Sophie, Emile finds it necessary to remind both himself and Sophie that though tied to Sophie as a lover, his duties as citizen take priority over his love. In short, Emile manages to maintain his autonomy both as man and as citizen though part of an interdependent and intimate relationship. In saying to Sophie that the "rights of humanity" (whatever they may be) are "more sacred" to him than his love for her, he ranks in order what he perceives as conflicting duties. Willing what is best for the common good will always take priority over his love for Sophie.

Singling out the conflict between duty and inclination, however, is only *one* possible way to interpret this story. We might identify with Emile and see his actions as completely justified, even honorable, had we not the benefit of an alternative perspective. In the person of Sophie, however, Rousseau offers the alternative perspective. Sophie does not accept the rules of the game as Emile lays them out. She fails to see a contradiction in her duty to the rights of humanity and the needs of those most dear to her. Sophie is moved by Emile's story of sacrifice, promises to love him forever, and suggests (to Emile's surprise) that they immediately visit the people Emile had helped. Once they arrive, Sophie knows exactly what to do:

> Her gentle and light hand knows how to get at everything that hurts them and to place their sore limbs in a more relaxed position. They feel relieved at her very approach. One would say that she guesses everything which hurts them. . . . She has the appearance and the grace, as well as the gentleness and the goodness of an angel. Emile is moved and contemplates her in silence. Man, love your companion. God gives her to you to console you in your pains, to relieve you in your ills. This is woman. (E, V:441–2)

Again, this passage could be read as yet another example of an excessively gendered portrayal of the roles of man and woman in the good society: man is a citizen who helps his fellow-citizens; woman waits silently, comforting all after the fact. Yet, although it is that, it is also much more. For though Sophie's place is constantly one of the shadows, the background, and the margins, her actions implicitly (and sometimes explicitly) challenge the model being put forth by Rousseau in his recommendation that Emile be considered the best citizen.

When we read this passage, we have to wonder at Emile's dismissal of Sophie's worry, his immediate announcement that no matter how close the two of them might be or become, the "rights of humanity" will always override his love for his future wife, the future mother of his children. This announcement plants a seed of doubt in the reader's mind about whether one must, indeed, rank these priorities. Is it necessarily the case that to love another person intimately automatically conflicts with one's duties as a citizen? Does an acknowledgment of love for a particular other (in this case Sophie) automatically threaten the duty we have toward others whom we don't know very well at all? Emile consistently puts abstract others (those whom he knows by recognizing the common in himself as the common in all) first, whereas Sophie looks for the peculiarities that distinguish people and make each unique, lovable or not.

Les Solitaires: Sophie's Potential Expanded and Denied

Sophie's way, what Sophie knows, becomes even more dangerous as the story of Emile and Sophie continues. In *Emile*, mirroring the argument Rousseau makes about the city as theatre in his *Letter to D'Alembert*, Emile and Sophie are constantly warned to avoid the big city. In fact, Emile and his tutor had already visited Paris searching for the ideal woman. Of course, their search was fruitless: Paris is no place for a virtuous woman. They came home unsatisfied, disappointed, and restless:

> We are sad and dreamy as we leave Paris. This city of chatter is not the place for us. Emile turns a disdainful eye toward this great city and says resentfully, "How many days lost in vain searches! Ah, the wife of my heart is not there. My friend, you knew it well." (E, V: 410)

Like a love that would foster mutual dependency, the "city of chatter" threatens Emile's vision of himself, his autonomy, his authenticity. The big city is full of people who might cause Emile to question his own vision of himself:

> In a big city, full of scheming, idle people without religion or principle, whose imagination, depraved by sloth, inactivity, the love of pleasure, and great needs, engenders only monsters and inspires only crimes; in a big city, . . . morals [manners] and honor are nothing because each,

easily hiding his conduct from the public eye, shows himself only by his reputation and is esteemed only for his riches. (LD'A, 58–9)

In a big city, people are known by what others think of them. Their "reputation" proceeds them. One is forced to live outside one's self, like a woman, in the opinion of others. Richard Sennett has remarked that though Rousseau hated urban public life, he was the most constant student of the city, arriving "at the first complete and probing theory of the modern city as an expressive milieu."[16] Here people are free from the duties of survival: they seek entertainment and leisure; they interact on the streets, in the cafés, on the boulevards. They are extremely sociable: they speak, listen, pay the greatest attention to one another's gestures and the way ideas are expressed. According to Rousseau, style seems almost as important as content in this milieu. The "art of conversation" blossoms.

Iris Marion Young commends the urban atmosphere as offering an alternative to the impasse between liberal individualism and communitarianism. Defining subjectivity as multiple and heterogeneous, as opposed to stable and transparent, Young argues that people cannot ever be fully autonomous or visibly transparent to others. We are always living and working in response and in connection with others in a way that makes "misunderstanding, rejection, withdrawal, and conflict" certainly as viable as outcomes to social intercourse as are mutual understanding and reciprocity.[17] It is these possibilities, which arise from the interactions of people with multiple understandings of themselves and multiple ways of expressing those desires (and multiple ways that they can be understood), that is the heart of political relations. Young describes and embraces the diversity of city life as an alternative to either liberal autonomy or community identity in words that are reminiscent of Rousseau's warnings *against* city life (and the *feminine* as the principle at the heart of city life). As Young puts it:

> City life is a vast, even infinite, economic network of production, distribution, transportation, exchange, communication, service provision, and amusement. City dwellers depend on the mediation of thousands of other people and vast organizational resources in order to accomplish their individual ends. City dwellers are thus together, bound to one

another, in what should be and sometimes is a single polity. Their being together entails some common problems and common interests, but they do not create a community of shared final ends, of mutual identification and reciprocity.[18]

In his condemnation of city life and his singling out of salon life as microcosm of the connections between femininity, urbanity, and difference, Rousseau vilifies this atmosphere as inauthentic and as completely lacking in seriousness. Yet, just as Rousseau is a serious student of the "city of chatter" he finds so threatening, he is also a serious student of femininity. He makes it clear that despite its frivolity, the "chatter" of women must be carefully and closely guarded. Like the city, women *are* a serious threat to the kind of community Rousseau is ostensibly attempting to create. Women's knowledge (exemplified here in Sophie's actions) directly challenges all that Rousseau argues is good, authentic, virtuous, even democratic. As Dena Goodman reminds us:

> The Enlightenment was not a game, and the salonnières were not simply ladies of leisure killing time. . . . Like the philosophes who gathered in their home, the salonnières were practical people who worked at tasks they considered productive and useful. They took themselves, their salons, and their guests very seriously.[19]

Just as Sophie does, we might add.

Had the story of Emile and Sophie ended with Rousseau's *Emile*, we might believe that Rousseau actually bought his own precepts and conclusions: that gender boundaries ensure a good community, that autonomy is absolutely essential in order to make decent moral and political choices, that his masculine vision of democracy (one where the general will rules all and each is forced to be free) is the one he finds most viable and desirable.

The story of Emile and Sophie does not, however, end so tidily. Rousseau reveals, even more powerfully than in *Emile* itself, his deep ambivalence about his own solutions in his tragic "conclusion," *Emile et Sophie, ou Les Solitaires*. Only two chapters of *Les Solitaires* were actually completed by Rousseau; these chapters take the form of letters written by Emile to his tutor. Judith Sklar notes the significance of this work, stating that "not a single theme of real importance to Rousseau is left out in these thirty-odd pages."[20] We learn immediately that Emile and Sophie have suffered many hardships, most importantly, the death of their young daughter and both of Sophie's parents. Sophie is devastated by these events. Her misery leads Emile to contemplate that which he had been so severely warned against: to travel to Paris to distract Sophie from her pain. As Rousseau had predicted, coming to Paris proves to be their downfall. The city had a poisonous effect on Emile's soul and his fate. Emile writes that upon establishing themselves in Paris, he began to undergo a revolution in himself that he found impossible to forestall. He was so worn by frivolous amusements that his heart lost strength, becoming, as he put it, incapable of heat and force (that is, he ceased to have an honest inner life). He was only happy where he was not and sought out everything only to quickly become bored. All his affections became tepid; he let go of his attachments, including his attachment to Sophie.

Tempted by Parisian women, Emile has an affair. Sophie, discarded by Emile, finds herself pregnant by another man. Emile, taught to love Sophie's honor more than Sophie herself, cannot accept Sophie's mistake (which was merely a response to Emile's own adultery) and blames her tyrannical power over him for his own subsequent misery. He rejects Sophie and plans an even sweeter revenge in having Sophie separated from their son. Rejected by Emile, separated from her son, and consumed by grief, Sophie gives up on life and dies.

Attempting to digest this story, one might argue that it merely confirms Rousseau's edicts: the city and certain kinds of women in the city (even Sophie in the city) threaten community. Even the small trio of Emile, Sophie, and their son fail to survive in such a corrupt environment. Scholars have argued that Rousseau's bias against the customs and manners of city life turn on his desire to preserve authenticity.[21] Underpinning this interpretation is a particular reading of the *Second Discourse* that indicates that for Rousseau, modern life always entails loss: we were once authentic and natural beings; we could communicate in an unmediated and transparent fashion; we were not slaves to *amour-propre*. Rousseau's goal in creating Emile is to create both a natural man and a citizen—a citizen who can know himself, communicate authentically, and legitimate a political arrangement that, as best as possible, preserves our original freedom. This argument, however, presumes that Rousseau thinks his goal is possible and that he has actually done it, that he has succeeded at some level in constructing such an authentic community in the midst of the modern world.

I contend, in contrast, that Rousseau's work points elsewhere. The dominant model put forth by Rousseau for the way citizens should act is Emile as manly citizen. But even Emile ends up unhappy. He is only able to preserve the precarious balance between his role as man/citizen and his interactions with others in the world by projecting what he knows of himself onto others. In the city, he is unable do this: Emile loses his sense of identity in the urban milieu. Unable to "read" himself, Emile fails to satisfactorily interact with others. At the same time, Rousseau presents us with an alternative model in the character of Sophie. Were it not for Emile's rejection of Sophie as a mother, wife, lover, and friend, Sophie might have basked in the city's more political offerings. It was Sophie, after all, who was educated to live in the eyes of others, even learn the hearts of others almost better than her own. Sophie might have been able to develop these talents in a political milieu that rewards the ability to engage with opposing, even incommensurable positions, listen and respond to arguments borne of competing ethical frameworks, and confront differences and make judgments in a critical and fair way.

In the end, Rousseau's "identity-based" solution fails at every level. Unable to "know" himself as a man, Emile loses himself as a citizen. The same would be true of Sophie, were she forced to fulfill the dictates of the male-envisioned feminine. But, as is clear from my reading of *Emile* in this chapter, neither Emile's nor Sophie's identities, even their most "natural" sexual identities, are either stable or authentic. Emile's performance as a man (and likewise Sophie's performance as a woman) is presumably critical for achieving republican community, yet the community completely disintegrates once the fiction of their identity lies exposed.

We are left with a number of lingering questions from our initial scrutiny of Rousseau's construction of gender identity. Though Rousseau himself is certain that gender boundaries do not exist in nature, he finds that he needs to create the *appearance of the natural*, inscribed on men's and women's bodies, in order to command discipline from the male citizens he says are necessary for republican community. But neither sexual identity nor republican community is successful. Keeping this in mind, I have tracked Sophie's manners and attributes as a possible democratic alternative suggested by Rousseau.

The feminine is closely tied with the urban and the theatrical in Rousseau's oeuvre, all of which signify an inauthentic *seeming to be* as opposed to an authentic being. Though Rousseau argues that *seeming to be* is dangerous to his political "solution" to the problem posed by the need to form a legitimate government, as we will see in the following chapter, both the social contract (exemplified by Clarens in *La Nouvelle Héloïse*) and alternative kinds of arrangements are based on performance. Yet Rousseau remains intrigued by the performance of the women he creates. Is it possible that he finds women's ways more promising for democratic practice?

3

The Dangerous Insider

Rousseau's Julie

•

Interpreters of Rousseau debate how best to categorize his thought. Descriptions range from radical democratic communitarian to dangerously misguided misogynist. No matter how one reads Rousseau's politics, a glaring inequality remains central to his work: the clear declaration that only men can and should be public citizens in the traditional sense. What, then, could possibly draw scholars committed to democracy and equality back to Rousseau's work? I have argued that when we look to Rousseau's women, an alternative conception of citizenship emerges. Drawing on the subversive feminine presence at the core of Rousseau's manly citizen, the alternative challenges liberal and communitarian concepts of politics, political space, political deliberation, and the way we understand the tension between our particular identities and our universal humanity.

In the previous chapter we noted that Sophie was taught differently than Emile. She was taught to live outside herself, in the opinion of others, in accordance with the ways of the theatrical, in terms of *seeming to be*. Confined to the private space, this way of behaving allowed Sophie certain kinds of knowledge to which Emile had no access—for instance, knowing the ways of peoples' hearts; understanding those who, for whatever reason, are not able to speak in the dominant discourse, yet want to be heard; understanding the value of emotion and commitment to particular others; successfully integrating commitment to those near and dear with commitment to citizenship in the larger sense. These attributes would have served Sophie well in the city, indeed in any community, had not Emile taken her son from her and rejected her as his lover. Emile's choice is a prime example of what Rousseau demands of his manly citizens: he must reject Sophie in the face of the transgression of her honor (her violation of the role of Woman) despite their desire to live together as lovers, friends, and parents. In *Les Solitaires*, Sophie and Emile both meet tragic fates (Sophie dies and Emile lives as a loner) solely and precisely because of what duty demands of the manly citizen.

As we will see in what follows, Rousseau's Julie is a Sophie in flesh and blood terms, a woman who actually could become the alternative to his manly citizen. In *La Nouvelle Héloïse*, the feminine presence disrupts all that Rousseau in other works (especially *Social Contract*, *The Government of Poland*, and *Letter to D'Alembert*) advocates as best for republican community: male solidarity, the festival as education for citizenry, rules against a "too intimate commerce" between men and women. All these direct Rousseau toward advocating a unilateral, provincial, and univocal public sphere that dictates proper behavior to everyone. Exploring the feminine in Rousseau allows me to more fully expand on his ambivalence concerning the price of such a community. When we adopt the perspective of Rousseau's women, alternatives to his social contract lie naked at the heart of his texts.

Readings of *Julie*

In *Fictions of Feminine Desire*, Peggy Kamuf reminds us that Julie is, for Rousseau, the "new Heloise." In this sense, Kamuf argues, Rousseau's book is meant to be a "fiction of closure: that of an imagined paternal identity preserved by a daughter's virtue."[1] At one level, the novel is supposed to represent Julie's transformation from daughter of the Baron d'Etange, keeper of the aristocratic order, to wife of Wolmar and mistress of Clarens, representative of the new republican alternative. It is quite difficult for Julie to make the sacrifice necessary for this transition: she must overcome her love for the petit bourgeois Saint-Preux. Unruly passion between the two lovers threatens to undermine both aristocratic and republican order. Saint-Preux redirects his passion to the fatherland (in terms of the small community of Clarens); Julie simply represses her passion in concentrating on her duties as wife of Wolmar and mother of his children.

A tidy and moral story, a glorification of sacrifice and virtue? According to the once dominant Kantian interpretation, yes: the autonomous morality of duty wins out over the heteronomy of happiness and feeling. This interpretation fails, however, to account for the ambivalence signified in the depth of Rousseau's attachment to his characters and to each of their varying perspectives. Noting that for the most part scholars of political and social theory have failed to take *The New Heloise* seriously (due to the split in English-speaking countries between Rousseau the political theorist and Rousseau the theorist of education, both of which ignore Rousseau's literary works), Alessandro Ferrara attempts to complicate the lessons of Rousseau's novel. He argues that "to the extent that a novel can be 'about' anything," it is "about the relation of self-realization to morality."[2] Posing an ethic of autonomy against an ethic of authenticity, Ferrara interprets Julie's dilemma as tragic in that it introduces a new kind of unsolvable conflict. Julie must choose between making her parents happy by marrying Wolmar (an autonomously chosen principle) and being true to her love for Saint-Preux (a not-yet-legitimate feeling because outside the realm of her parents' consent). For Ferrara, this dilemma suggests that

> sometimes moral choices may have to be made in which the right solution is to side with our feelings, as opposed to our ethical principles, if the feelings in question are bound up with the cohesion of our identity ... Our act would then be justified solely by our considered judgment about the relation of the feeling at issue to our identity.[3]

In this interpretation, Ferrara makes Julie's dilemma of identity key to what Rousseau wants us to learn from his work. Rousseau teaches that we must act authentically against the rigid morality of autonomy, yet we cannot do so until the "secret principle" of our hearts is brought completely to consciousness.[4] For Julie, this does not occur until the end of the novel when she realizes that, despite her desire to succeed in her marriage with Wolmar and conquer her former passion, she has indeed loved Saint-Preux all along.

Though Ferrara's interpretation is more subtle and insightful than the Kantian interpretation (especially in its recognition that Rousseau does not rigidly identify autonomy as key to morality and thus does not consistently side with characters like Emile and Wolmar), he continues to find authenticity and identity as coherent and viable principles in Rousseau's work. In the previous chapter, I questioned the stability of both concepts in Rousseau's *Emile*. I argued that when we look at Rousseau's attempt to create gender roles, both identity and authenticity become significantly more complicated within Rousseau's own terms. Following on this line of thought in *The New Heloise*, I will map the creation of gender and Rousseau's consistent identification with the feminine. This path allows me to trace Rousseau's ambivalence concerning his own political solutions.

Lisa Disch offers a compelling interpretation of Rousseau's novel.[5] Focusing on the friendship between Julie and her cousin Claire in order to read this "friendship story" against the dominant "virtue story," Disch articulates a powerful Rousseauian critique of Enlightenment thought. Central to this critique is Rousseau's definition of (and preference for) taste as a kind of reason that, rather than claiming an Archimedean point, is situated in contextual thinking. Though Disch argues that this counter-story is a clearly articulated and viable alternative to the virtue story, she says that it ultimately fails to achieve its potential. Disch concludes that Julie fails to find Claire's sympathy convincing and chooses instead, like Sophie, to live in the gaze of men. The potentially subversive components (the friendship between the two women, the model of taste as a clear replacement for a model of finding the common within one's self), then, are neatly contained.

Peggy Kamuf and Juliet Flower MacCannell are not quite as certain about that containment. Kamuf reads *Julie, or the New Heloise* as a story of subterfuge, of the creation of what she calls an "aqueduct" in the form of Julie's desire, which "doubles, and undermines, the august singularity of the paternal autochthon."[6] Going even further (and fruitfully so) MacCannell argues that Rousseau sets up the "rational" model at Clarens, denies Julie's sexual desire, and kills her in the end so that we will find the results monstrous. As MacCannell states in *The Regime of the Brother* (whose title refers to her characterization of the "postpatriarchy" inside the "fraternal empire"):

> I think Rousseau intended his depiction to be a critique of a fundamental fantasy of the Regime of the Brother: concocting a conscious and ar-

tificial re-enactment of the "best" of patriarchy while acknowledging it as only a fantasy, a pure product of imagination and will . . . And it is dreadful . . . Julie's death dramatizes the critical failure—once again the woman's failure to be able to live her own desire, her own identity as anything other than a male fantasy.[7]

Following these feminist studies of *La Nouvelle Héloïse* (Disch, Kamuf, and MacCannell), I will argue that while MacCannell is right in claiming that Rousseau laments the demise of Julie to warn against the denial of women's desire, he simultaneously points us toward an alternative politics where this denial (and all it implies) would be unacceptable. I will build on my study of Sophie to extend Rousseau's construction of, and identification with, femininity (in this novel embodied in Julie, Claire, and, at times, in Saint-Preux) in order to begin to chart the alternative. Revealed far more explicitly in *The New Heloise* than in *Emile* are the ways Rousseau indicates that women view the world and the way, in particular, that women's desire might alter our sense of what is moral, how to judge, and how to be citizens within a political community.

Saint-Preux, the Manly; Julie, the Alternative

In *Emile, or On Education*, one of Rousseau's goals was to educate Emile from an early age to be both man and citizen. We have noted the failure of both identities. In *La Nouvelle Héloïse*, Rousseau tries something even more difficult: rather than starting with an uncorrupted boy child as his raw material for citizenship, he looks to a man at the margins of society, Saint-Preux, and a man already considered an upstanding citizen (but not of the ideal society), Wolmar. Neither of these men are able to be convincing or compelling citizens because neither knows how to love.

Recall that the personal and the political are intricately connected in Rousseau's oeuvre, and that Rousseau finds stories of love far more convincing than moral tales. This is why, in his *Letter to D'Alembert*, he opposes the introduction of a theater in Geneva: citizens who have been taught good morals and virtues, who have been taught to keep their gender identities "straight" and to love their fatherland above all else, would be far too affected by the love interest in the theater. The personal appeals to us above all else; when we see and identify with persons in love, we are apt to sympathize with their dilemmas even if fulfilling passion means defying gender roles and the dictates of the fatherland. Rousseau writes that "the harm for which the theatre is reproached is not precisely that of inspiring criminal passions but of disposing the soul to feelings which are too tender and which are later satisfied at the expense of virtue" (LD'A, 51).

That being the case, what are we to make of the fact that Rousseau's men inspire nothing but contempt, whereas his women inspire sympathy? What are we to learn from the fact that his men do not know how to love, that they consistently sacrifice love for duty, and that his women suffer immeasurably for these "manly" decisions in favor of virtue and duty? None of Rousseau's men are able to truly love in a way that inspires the tender feelings of heart that Rousseau so admires, in a way that would inspire great sacrifice without hesitation, in a way that the whole world is changed in light of that love. For example, before Emile ever met Sophie, he "loved" her. But this love was abstract. His tutor presented him with an image of Woman, of the perfect woman, to nourish his judgment, to be certain that Emile would be able to distinguish between mutual dependency (whereby he would continually be beholden to the opposite sex) and authentic autonomy (whereby Sophie varies her performances as acquiescent wife and masterful mistress with Emile in control of reading her "bodily" signs as to what she desires). As we saw in the short but tragic *Les Solitaires*, Sophie's "honor" is far more important to Emile than any emotional needs or genuine desire (or lack thereof). When Emile meets Sophie, "he loves a lovable object who is even more lovable for her character than for her person" (E, V:419).

Linda M. G. Zerilli calls the chaste image of Woman that replaces actual women "the celestial object." She explains the idea of the "celestial object" in reference to Alfred Binet's credit to Rousseau for "a form of fetishism that substituted the relic for and preferred it to the woman to whom it originally belonged."[8] This fetishism is brilliantly displayed by Saint-Preux as part of performing his manhood. As it turns out, performing one's manhood is shockingly dissimilar from actually loving another person. Julie accuses Saint-Preux of only being able to love her in the abstract, as the object of *his* desire. In a perverse demonstration of the old adage "absence makes the heart grow fonder," Saint-Preux gets most excited about Julie when the real Julie, complete with foibles, is safely at a distance.

This can be seen, for example, when Julie sends Saint-Preux "a sort of amulet that lovers are wont to wear" (J, II:XX, 216). Saint-Preux's letter to Julie upon receiving this love object appeals to prurient interests. He excitedly recounts to Julie that "a sort of sensuality" seized his imagination; he shifted the object from hand to hand such that "one would have thought it was burning them" (J, II:XXII, 228). He reports that he rushed home from the post, fondling the object all the way, dreaming of its "volume," its "weight," and the "tone of [Julie's] letter" (J, II:XXII, 228). Upon arrival at his lodging, Saint-Preux is free to open the package:

> Finally, I arrive, I hurry, I shut myself in my room, I sit down out of breath, I place a trembling hand on the seal. O the first effect of the talisman! I felt my heart throb with every paper I removed, and soon found myself so greatly oppressed that I was forced to catch a moment's breath at the last layer. . . . Julie! . . . O my Julie! . . . (J, II:XXII, 229).

Exhausted, Saint-Preux ends his encounter with the day's mail collapsing in an orgasmic swoon onto the bed.

In another instance, Saint-Preux writes to Julie that "a frantic love feeds on fantasies," and that it is quite possible, even "easy" to "decoy intense desires with the most frivolous objects!" (J, II:XVI, 197). He claims to receive Julie's letters with the "same transports [her] presence would have evoked, and in the exaltation of my joy a mere piece of paper stood me in stead of you" (J, II:XVI, 197). Appalled by her lover's delight in his solitary experiences of her, Julie admonishes Saint-Preux:

> I fear these deceiving raptures, so much the more dangerous when the imagination which excites them has no limits, and I am more afraid that you are insulting your Julie in your very love for her. . . . What do you enjoy when you are the only one to enjoy it? These solitary, sensual pleasures are lifeless pleasures. . . . Sensual man, will you never know how to love?[9]

As we read on, it becomes even more apparent that Saint-Preux does not know how to love in the way Julie desires. Saint-Preux's self-absorption (stemming from his education as manly citizen) encourages him to think solely of what he desires, mapping his own desire onto the "objects" around him.[10] When he is not imagining Julie as a lover in the form of an amulet or piece of paper, Saint-Preux imagines Julie as property. Wolmar too considers Julie "property" transferred from her father to himself (J, IV:VII, 353).

Warned to avoid mutual dependency that is fostered through love, Rousseau's men imagine women as objects, projecting their own desires onto a fantasy of Woman primarily because they fear an attachment to real women. Like Julie's father, Wolmar's goal is to "live nearly independently within the bonds of wedlock" (J, IV:XII, 404). This lack of affect, noted by Julie as Wolmar's "self-control and moderation," manifests itself in a six-year silence on Wolmar's part in regard to "his family" and "his person" (J, IV:XII, 401).

The relationships between the sexes portrayed in *La Nouvelle Héloïse* are reminiscent of those in *Emile*. Recall that Emile too was cautioned to avoid mutual dependency in his relationship with Sophie. Jean-Jacques, Emile's tutor, had cautioned Emile that a too-close attachment to Sophie would threaten his autonomy, especially in terms of his ability to make good judgments. Recall that when Jean-Jacques felt Emile had become too close to Sophie, he insisted that Emile travel around the world to assure himself that he could live easily without the one he loved. In another instance, Emile's tutor reminded his student never to allow Sophie's opinions or desires to dictate what he considered good and moral behavior. When absorbed in Sophie's love, Emile faltered. His dependency on Sophie's approval caused his heart great distress, undermining his ability to conduct himself as a manly citizen. When reminded by his tutor never to allow Sophie's presence to have such an effect, Emile expressed relief. The tutor reminded Emile that for him to act autonomously was the best for Sophie as well: "His decent heart is delighted that in order to please Sophie he has to do exactly what he would do on his own if Sophie did not exist or if he were not in love with her" (E, V:423).

In contrast, Rousseau's women find that the ability to make good moral judgments is intractably tied to commitments to others. Confused by their dilemma, Saint-Preux and Julie wonder what to do: defy the father in the name of their love, or suppress their passion to conform to society's version of virtue? Julie begs Saint-Preux to follow her lead in making a decision in this matter:

> I admit I am the younger; but have you never noticed that if reason is generally weaker and sooner to wane in women, it is also formed earlier, just as a frail sunflower grows and dies quicker than an oak. We find ourselves, from the tenderest age, assigned such a dangerous trust, that the responsibility of preserving it soon awakens our judgment, and an excellent way to see clearly the consequences of things is to feel intensely the risks they cause us to run. (J, I:XI, 45)

Claiming that her reason is more fully developed than his, Julie explains in even more compelling terms why Saint-Preux should allow her to steer their relationship: Saint-Preux should defer to his lover because it is Julie who is able to think of both of them, and of their commitments to their family and society, *all at the same time*. Saint-Preux is only able to think of himself. Julie argues that "the opinion of whichever of us least distinguishes his own happiness from the other's is the one to be preferred" (J, I:XI, 45).

Claire also makes judgments that factor in her responsibility to others. When Julie first informs Claire of her love for Saint-Preux, Claire expresses extreme anxiety about the situation but promises not to betray Julie's confidence. She acknowledges that "many would find it more honest to reveal it; maybe they would be right" (J, I:VII, 37). It would be more honest in that it is the naked truth, but, Claire reasons, it is a truth that would harm a number of people, her beloved Julie included. Claire wants no part in an "honesty that betrays faith, trust, friendship" (J, I:VII, 37). This kind of contextual model for moral reasoning is clearly an alternative, and a subversive one at that, to the autonomous decision making required of manly citizens. Later on in the novel, learning that Julie has taken sick due to the absence of her lover, Claire is the one willing to call Saint-Preux back to her side. When Julie questions her own worth in society's eyes, Claire assures her that just because she has lost her virginity, she is not less worthy in the eyes of her friend:

Is genuine love meant to degrade the soul? Let not a single fault that love has committed deprive you of that noble enthusiasm for honesty and beauty, which always raised you above yourself. Is a spot visible on the sun? How many virtues do you still possess for one that has become tainted? Will that make you any less sweet, less sincere, less modest, less generous? Will you be any less worthy, in a word, of all our praise? Honor, humanity, friendship, pure love, will these be any less dear to your heart? Will you have any less love for those virtues you no longer possess? No, dear and good Julie, while pitying you, your Claire worships you. (J, I:XXX, 81)

Further expounding on the politics of love, Rousseau indicates that women's way of loving as expressed through contextualized reasoning could even be considered a demonstration of better judgment. Recall that Julie, not Saint-Preux or Wolmar, consistently knows how to love, and in doing so makes good decisions. Early on in their exchange of letters, Saint-Preux complains to Julie that though he has written to his beloved Julie and there has been plenty of time for her to respond, he has not received any word. He claims that "there is no possible dire reason for its delay that [his] troubled spirit does not imagine" (J, I:XIX, 57). Julie replies that Saint-Preux's imagination has forged far ahead of his reason:

> Your two letters reached me at the same time because the Courier, who comes only once a week, set out only with the second. It takes a certain amount of time to deliver letters; it takes more for my agent to bring me mine in secret, and the Courier does not return from here the day after his arrival. Thus all told, we need eight days, when the Courier's day is well chosen, to receive replies from each other; I explain this in order to calm once and for all your impatient petulance. While you are declaiming against fortune and my negligence, you see that I am adroitly gathering information about whatever can assure our correspondence and anticipate your uncertainties. I leave you to decide on which side the most tender care is to be found. (J, I:XX, 58)

Loving care, for Julie, means attention to assuring their love and happiness. This is manifested most concretely in maintaining correspondence between the two lovers if necessary, but ideally in arranging for their physical proximity. Just as Julie arranges the rendezvous for their first kiss and manipulates circumstances to provide for subsequent amorous engagements, she constantly erodes barriers and seeks pathways in order for their love to continue. Saint-Preux, in contrast, busily occupies himself with imaginary raptures of Julie and the never-ending task of preserving his own "honor." In one of their many exchanges, Julie informs her lover that following her father's inquiry into Saint-Preux's background and circumstances—which Julie's father discovers are "honest" as opposed to "noble" (the death knell for any chance of a marriage between the two as interpreted by the class-conscious father)—her father insists that Saint-Preux be paid for his tutoring of his daughter, else he be dismissed. Fueling the importance of Saint-Preux's reply to this request, Julie confides that the father's pride has been offended by the tutor's refusal of payment. Saint-Preux, as should have been expected, immediately refuses any payment. Hence, he places his own honor above the consequence of being dismissed as tutor of Julie, seemingly disregarding the inevitable consequence—separation from her:

> I distinguish in what is called honor, that which is drawn from public opinion, and that which derives from self-esteem. The former consists in vain prejudices more tossed than a windblown wave; the latter has its basis in the eternal truths of morality. Worldly honor can be advantageous to fortune, but it does not penetrate into the soul and has no influence on true happiness. Genuine honor on the contrary constitutes its very essence, because only in it can that permanent sentiment of inner satisfaction be found which alone can make a thinking being happy. Let us, my Julie, apply these principles to your question; it will quickly be resolved. (J, I:XXIV, 69)

Honor, it turns out, is served by refusing payment. Were he to accept payment, he would be given the absurd responsibility of guarding Julie's chastity, obviously impossible at this point. Saint-Preux concludes:

> Here duty, reason, even love, all speak with an unmistakable voice. If I must choose between honor and you, my heart is prepared to lose you: it loves you too much, O Julie, to preserve you at that price. (J, I:XXIV, 71)

Here we see once again that Rousseau's men, when performing their manhood, define love in a way that eschews relationship, that pits duty against inclination, the heart and reason "endlessly at war" (J, I:XXVI, 73). Julie, on the other hand, demonstrates alternative definitions of love, reason, and duty. Saying that she will not interfere in Saint-Preux's decision to refuse payment and to be dismissed and take leave of her, Julie is also quick to point out that in pitting duty against passion and presumably choosing "honor" to commend his love, Saint-Preux has chosen the easy way out in terms of his reputation without due consideration of the consequences for their relationship. Julie is aghast at Saint-Preux's inability to distinguish between, and then intertwine, commitment to a lover and commitment to duty. She finds this offense revealed in the *manner* in which Saint-Preux's letter to her was composed. She argues that his letter was written as if it would be on public display:

> Really, how could you fail to sense that there is quite a difference between writing for the public and writing to one's mistress? Does not love, so timorous, so scrupulous, demand more deference than does propriety? Could you be unaware that such style is not to my taste, and were you trying to annoy me? (J, I:XXV, 71)

Later on in the same letter, Julie's annoyance and rebuke turns to sadness in considering the consequences of Saint-Preux's selfish decision. As Julie remarks:

> It is the persistence of sufferings that makes their weight unbearable, and the soul bears sharp pains more easily than prolonged sadness. That, my friend, is the hard sort of battle we shall henceforth have to wage: it is not heroic actions that duty requires of us, but a still more heroic resistance to unrelenting sufferings. (J, I:XXV, 71)

As for the consequences of Saint-Preux's "honorable" decision? Julie must "repress [her] tears," "must smile when [she] feel[s] like dying" (J, I:XXV, 72).

Saint-Preux's practice of "loving" Julie prepares him well for his eventual acceptance into the community at Clarens. As we shall see, despite her love for Saint-Preux, Julie eventually is persuaded by her father (in light of her mother's death) to marry Wolmar and attempt to live a conventional life as wife and mother. Many years after Julie's marriage to Wolmar, he "tests" the passion of Julie and her former lover by asking Saint-Preux to live at Clarens as tutor to Wolmar and Julie's children. Unlike Julie, who is never able to fully conform to her husband's authority, Saint-Preux quickly learns Wolmar's ways and is "cured" of any residual passion he might have had for his lover. When Saint-Preux is initially summoned to Clarens, he doubts his ability to suppress his love for Julie. He worries aloud in his letter to Claire:

> Can I change the fact that a thousand flames once devoured me? How am I by imagination alone to distinguish what is from what was? And how am I to think of her as a friend whom I never saw but as a lover? (J, IV:III, 341)

Surprisingly, then, the "cure" works almost immediately. Saint-Preux's initial glimpse of Julie sparks his memory of her as a lover. But moments later, when Saint-Preux sees Julie surrounded by her children, he sees her in a whole new light, this time as Madame de Wolmar, Monsieur de Wolmar's wife:

> It was a materfamilias I was embracing; I saw her surrounded by her Husband and children; this awed me. I saw in her a dignified mien that had not struck me at first; I felt obliged to have a new sort of respect for her; her familiarity was almost a burden; as beautiful as she seemed to me I would have kissed the hem of her dress more willingly than her cheek. From that instant, in a word, I knew that neither she nor I were the same, and I began in earnest to augur well for myself. (J, IV:VI, 348)

The Price of Wolmar's Regime

Scholars have noted that if we take Clarens as representative of Rousseau's ideal community, Rousseau's commitment to democratic practice is far less convincing than it might otherwise be. Jean Starobinski, for example, notes the contrast between the "democratic ideal of *The Social Contract* and the still feudal structure of the community at Clarens."[11] Joel Schwartz points out the obvious in this case: "Clarens is a highly inegalitarian society . . . in fact a despotism, as Rousseau makes perfectly evident."[12] The most important distinguishing characteristics of Clarens include presumption of transparent conversation between all (Wolmar says the society must be completely "open"—no hidden secrets); rules against a too intimate commerce between the sexes (we see this most clearly in the separation of male from female servants who come together only for festivals and the like); suppression of romantic love in favor of arranged marriage (exemplified between Julie and Wolmar, as well as in arrangements made for servants); and the enforcement of a model of reasoned dialogue and political/moral judgment that claims to treat all the same yet makes traitors of those who do not share the common experience. Rousseau's ambivalence about Clarens is buttressed by the many possible readings of the novel. From the perspective of Wolmar, and even of Saint-Preux, we might argue that Rousseau endorses his most severe prescriptions from his *Letter to D'Alembert*, most important among them that men can only conduct serious discourse amongst men:

> By themselves, the men, exempted from having to lower their ideas to the range of women and to clothe reason in gallantry, can devote themselves to grave and serious discourse without fear of ridicule. They dare to speak of country and virtue without passing for windbags; they even dare to be themselves without being enslaved to the maxims of a magpie (LD'A, 105).

What do men discuss outside the disruptive desire of women? In line with Rousseau's preference for transparent communication, at Clarens an atmosphere of "openness" must prevail. Wolmar reasons that since he observes "composedly and disinterestedly" he "scarcely err[s] in [his] judgments" (J, IV:XII, 403). His philosophy is such that:

> A single precept of morality can do for all the others; it is this: Never do nor say anything that thou does not wish everyone to see and hear. (J, IV:VI, 349)

Saint-Preux describes the effect that this single moral precept has on the conduct of everyone who lives at Clarens:

> All these vain subtleties are unknown in this house, and the great art of masters to make their domestics as they wish them is to show themselves to them as they are. Their conduct is always candid and open, because they do not fear lest their acts belie their words. As they do not have for themselves a moral different from the one they wish to impart to others, they have no need to be circumspect in what they say; a word that foolishly escapes them does not overturn the principles they have endeavored

to establish. They do not indiscreetly reveal all their business, but they freely state their maxims. At table, out strolling, in private or in front of everyone, they always maintain the same language. (J, IV:X, 385)

Everyone at Clarens is forced to act as if their hearts and minds were completely on display. All privacy has been effaced; all is openly revealed. The "openness," however, obscures all the secrets being kept. Forced to speak in a language that does not express her thoughts, feelings, or desires, Julie becomes unable to speak or listen at all; in fact, she kills herself in the end. As Lisa Disch notes, when one considers Wolmar's cool reason in light of its effect on Julie, it begins to look far more like punishment, discipline, and "cruel disregard for Julie's feelings" than like "perfect impartiality" or justice.[13] "The authority [Wolmar] wields is perverse both for its universalism, which erases Julie's feelings, and for its dogmatism, which makes it impossible for her to resist Wolmar's test without incriminating herself."[14] Had Julie chosen to recognize Claire's friendship as replacement for the love of a husband, Disch argues, Wolmar's cruel authority over Julie might have been subverted.

Both Starobinski and Schwartz emphasize that the success of Clarens as a community is dependent on the state of mind of its inhabitants such that though clearly unequal and differentiated, they believe they are equal contributing members. Most surprising in their analyses, though, is the interpretation that Julie "rules" this society and holds it together. Joel Schwartz's analysis of Rousseau's sexual politics rests on this assumption: Rousseau believes women to be both sexual and political (far more inclined to interest themselves in theatricality and domination—politics being our attempt to dominate one another), while men, or at least a few good men, might be able to "transcend the domination characteristic of politics and sexuality."[15] For Schwartz, Julie "rules" Clarens precisely because of her sexuality. He points out that Rousseau's ambivalence concerning sexuality dictates that women have considerable sexual power, and thus contact between the sexes should be avoided and vigorously policed. According to Schwartz:

> *Julie* tells the story of a woman's employment of authority. Women such as Julie use their authority to fashion men according to their feminine desires.[16]

Yet how can we assert that Julie's desire "fashions" Clarens in light of the fact that her unfulfilled desire leaves her unable to fight for her life? Soon after learning that Wolmar has invited her ex-lover into their home to live permanently, Julie plunges into an icy lake to save her child. She never recovers from the fever brought on by the "accident." How are we to read the centrality of Julie's role, both before and after her death?

Julie certainly is the "glue" that holds Clarens together. She is the pivotal figure at Clarens: the servants, the children, Wolmar, Saint-Preux, and Claire all direct their attention and concern to Julie. Even the structure of the letters and the title of the book place Julie as the main event. Before her death, Julie elaborates explicit and detailed rules concerning the direction and maintenance of the household in her absence. In one of the last letters of the novel, Wolmar explains at length the "long monologue" in the course of which Julie "wrote her testament" into his heart (J, VI:XI, 581). This influence over the household and the emotions of those within the household suggests that Julie exerted some control over important aspects of her own life and the lives of others.

At the same time, however, the image of Woman as well as the labor of women maintains the community as male-centered without any acknowledgment of women's autonomous desire and subjectivity—indeed, without women's autonomous participation. Julie is passed from her father to Wolmar and used as a suture between Wolmar and Saint-Preux. Her destiny could be read as "paradigmatic of a structure termed by anthropologists 'the exchange of women.'" Victoria Wohl elaborates:

> In the broadest sense, the term refers to the movement of a woman between two men as a bride, a gift, or . . . a prize. Whether the exchange is amicable . . . or hostile, . . . the transferal of a woman between two men constitutes the social world, generating bonds between the men and defining their social identities.[17]

Because Schwartz emphasizes the perspective of Rousseau's men, he argues that women have sexual power. When we focus on Rousseau's women, however, we notice women's *lack* of agency and control over the situation. I find it fascinating that Rousseau writes so convincingly about Julie's *discontent* (her *lack*, as it were). Once Julie marries Wolmar and becomes a part of the community of Clarens, she is forced to change her way of interacting with others. Instead of listening to each person alone, considering each perspective, and making everyone feel as if they each were uniquely important to her, Julie is forced to take on the ways of Wolmar and the rules of conduct imposed at Clarens. I maintain that Julie *herself* recognizes that she is unhappy at Clarens and that Rousseau's story demands that we strongly empathize with her grief. Though it goes against the rules of society and the rules of Wolmar, Julie sustains her desire for Saint-Preux while simultaneously trying to displace this desire onto passionate love for her children. Though Julie writes to Claire that her "status of wife and mother uplifts" her soul and sustains her "against the remorse" of her "earlier condition" (J, IV:I, 330), she also complains that Wolmar "does not respond enough to me for my fancy" (J, IV:I, 328). She argues that her husband's affection for herself and for their children is "too reasonable" (J, IV:I, 328). Julie says to Claire that she desires "a friend, a mother who is as dotty as me about my children and her own" (J, IV:I, 328).

From these statements, it seems quite clear that Julie is completely aware that her desire as a woman is not being fulfilled within the confines of Clarens. She tries to fill the gap with the love of her children, yet she remains unhappy and listless. Luce Irigaray writes that this is a typical response for a woman within the economy of male desire:

> If woman is asked to sustain, to revive, man's desire, the request neglects to spell out what it implies as to the value of her own desire. A desire of which she is not aware, moreover, at least not explicitly. But one whose force and continuity are capable of nurturing repeatedly and at length all the masquerades of "femininity" that are expected of her. It is true that she still has the child, in relation to whom her appetite for touch, for contact, has free rein, unless it is already lost, alienated by the taboo against touching of a highly obsessive civilization. Otherwise her pleasure will find, in the child, compensations for and diversions from the frustrations that she too often encounters in sexual relations per se. Thus maternity fills the gaps in a repressed female sexuality.[18]

But for Julie, love for the children, especially when not shared with Wolmar, is not enough. Wolmar seems to suspect (and certainly fear) Julie's discontent. It is as if any recognition of her autonomous feminine desire would lead explicitly and undeniably to a subversion of the Enlightenment order Wolmar has worked so diligently to create at Clarens. When Julie admits to Wolmar that she had loved Saint-Preux, Wolmar, in keeping with his cruel punishment of openly revealing all to everyone, invites Saint-Preux into their home to live with them and be tutor to their children. It is as if when he recognizes Julie's desire and frustration, rather than listen to her, he punishes her. This is the final act that proves too much for Julie to bear.

Notice again that Wolmar's values and way of understanding others is quite similar to Emile's. He takes what he knows of himself, assumes that it is common to all, and places it onto all around him. Any hint of difference is tinged with darkness, intrigue, secrecy, and chaos. As Saint-Preux observes of Clarens, at the table Wolmar (and Julie forced to act like Wolmar in his presence) "openly proclaim all their maxims . . . no matter what the situation, no matter who is speaking . . . their language is always the same." Wolmar invites Saint-Preux into their home to "cure" the lovers of their passion and to keep "open" conversation alive in the same, univocal, spirit. Anyone who speaks differently, or who disrupts the conversation as structured by Wolmar, must necessarily be banned from the community. Wolmar is inherently suspicious of what takes place outside of his vision, untouched by the order he imposes by his presence. When Julie, during her last few days of life, requests for Claire to sleep with her in the same bed, Wolmar is crazed by the fear of their potential intimacy. "As for me, I was sent off," he recounts (J, VI:XI, 582). Despite the fact that he "genuinely needed rest," Wolmar remained uneasy all night long. Explicitly he proclaims his worry over Julie's health; implicitly he worries about what exactly transpired between the two women:

> I was up early. Anxious to learn what had taken place during the night, at the first sound I heard I entered the bedroom. From Madame d'Orbe's condition the night before, I gauged the despair I would find her in and the rantings I would witness. Upon entering I saw her seated in an armchair, haggard and pale, or rather livid, her eyes leaden and almost lifeless; but she was gentle, quiet, she spoke little, and did all she was told, without answering. As for Julie, she appeared less weak than the night before, her voice was steadier, her gestures more animated; she

seemed to have taken on her Cousin's animation. I easily recognized from her color that this apparent improvement was the effect of fever: but I also saw glimmering in her eyes I know not what secret joy that might have contributed to it, the cause of which I could not determine. (J, VI:XI, 582–583)

Could the "secret joy" glimmering in Julie's eyes be attributed to a lesbian liaison with Claire? Wolmar starts to worry that he has never known Julie, that she has never been herself in his presence. It is odd that this should worry such a man as Wolmar, given his own rules. With Julie lying on her deathbed, Wolmar accuses her of secretly welcoming her death:

> Julie, my dear Julie! You have cut me to the heart: alas, you waited until very late! Yes, I continued, seeing that she looked at me with surprise; I have figured you out; you are delighted to be dying; you are more than happy to be leaving me. (J, VI:XI, 590)

Julie responds that "it is true"—that she is dying content, based on the knowledge that she is still "worthy" of being Wolmar's spouse (J, VI:XI, 590). Her answer to Wolmar reveals that she has maintained her virtue as a wife to the bitter end. But the limits imposed on her desire to maintain her stature and respect as wife to Wolmar have rendered her life unworthy of completion. She chooses death as a better option than the closed community of Clarens. She singles out her friendship with Claire as the one blessing that she alone was granted by heaven:

> I was a woman, and a woman was my friend. It caused us to be born at the same time; it placed in our inclinations an accord that has never been belied; it made our hearts for each other, it united us from the crib, I have kept her my whole life long, and her hand closes my eyes. Find another example like it on earth, and I will no longer boast of anything. What wise counsel has she not given me? From what perils has she not saved me? From what ills did she not console me? What would I have been without her? (J, VI:XI, 594)

Claire, however, is left behind. She is devastated at the prospect of life without Julie. Left alone in the world of men, Claire loses herself in the process. Her grief is profoundly alien to Wolmar. Describing her reaction to Julie's death, Wolmar writes:

Once I recovered from the initial shock I inquired after Madame d'Orbe. I learned that she had to be carried to her room, and even locked in: for at every moment she returned to Julie's, threw herself upon her body, warmed it with hers, endeavored to revive it, pressed it, clung to it in a sort of rage, called it loudly by a thousand passionate names, and sated her despair with all these pointless efforts. When I entered, I found her completely out of her mind, seeing nothing, hearing nothing, recognizing no one, rolling around on the floor wringing her hands and biting the legs of the chairs, murmuring some extravagant words in a muted voice, then at long intervals uttering piercing cries that made one start. (J, VI:XI, 602)

Practiced in the science of manly citizenship, Wolmar has no experience with which he can understand the depth and intensity of Claire's grief. His own grief being much more contained, he is at pains to understand the entire community's desire to bring Julie back from the dead. The strength of their desire is such that they believe Julie's father, who in his own despair thought he saw Julie's dead body "turn her eyes, look at him, nod to him" (J, VI:XI, 604). At this exclamation of Julie's "recovery," all have desire to believe:

It took no more than that; everyone came running, the neighbors, the poor whose lamentations rang in the air, they all exclaimed, she is not dead! The rumor spread and grew: the populace fond of the supernatural avidly took up the news; they believed it as they desired it; . . . I had arrived at the height of this fermentation. I soon recognized that it was impossible to talk reason to the multitude, that if I had the door closed and the body borne to the grave a tumult might ensue, that I would at the least pass for a parricidal husband who was having his wife buried alive, and that I would be held in horror by the whole countryside. I resolved to wait. (J, VI:XI, 604)

Why We Should Listen to Women

In analyzing women's relationship to communities, Susan Bickford has suggested that "an antifoundational thinker like Foucault, who is explicitly concerned with 'how human beings are made subjects,' might prove useful for feminists and others concerned with subjugation and transformation."[19] As I described in the chapter dealing explicitly with

Sophie, human beings are made subjects in Rousseau's oeuvre by enact-
ing and embodying the traits of their gender. In placing masculinist discourse in the public and feminine discourse in the private realm, Rousseau seems to believe that he has secured the smooth functioning of the
social contract. We don't have to listen to women, or listen to women
listening to others, à la the dominant interpretation of Rousseau, because women simply don't count in public discourse. Foucault claims,
in contrast, that what makes the excluded and the marginal *worth listen-*
ing to is precisely their difference from, and marginalization in terms of,
the dominant discourse: "[F]or there to be a sense in listening to them
and in searching for what they want to say, it is sufficient that they exist
and that they have against them so much which is set up to silence
them."[20]

Yet though Rousseau claims that women aren't worth listening to, he
gives them a lot to say, and he frames what women say in a way that
makes their statements quite compelling as an alternative to his own arguments. Just as in listening to what Sophie says, we begin to sketch an
alternative way of thinking, knowing, and judging, in listening to Julie
and Claire the same is true. Describing herself, Claire claims that she is
"a sort of monster" (J, I:LXIV, 146), ignoring the ways she is supposed
to behave in favor of defining her own course. Like Sophie, both Julie
and Claire are products of their social and cultural history. They have
been taught, for better or for worse, to "perform" their gender (with
Claire defying the rules she finds most obnoxious). Also like Sophie, Julie is an actress: she works at seeing, listening, and responding to those
around her. Recall that Sophie lives in the opinions of others; she deliberately makes other people feel recognized; everyone leaves the dinner
party thinking that Sophie has thought only of them. Julie has developed some of these same skills of communication, making everyone
feel they are her private and intimate friends. In the first letter that
Saint-Preux writes to Julie, the one in which he reveals his love for her,
he exclaims:

> No, fair Julie; your charms had dazzled my eyes, never would they have
> led my heart astray without the stronger charm that animates them. It is
> that touching combination of such lively sensibility and unfailing gen-
> tleness, it is that tender pity for all the sufferings of others, it is that

sound judgment and exquisite taste that draw their purity from the soul's own, it is, in a word, the attractions of the sentiments far more than those of the person that I worship in you. (J, I:I, 26)

Likewise, Claire notes that it is not Julie's beauty or her grace or the talent of pleasing that makes her the center of any community and draws others toward her. It is the "gift of loving" that makes Julie loved, "something undefinably seductive that is not merely pleasing, but affecting, and attracts all hearts" (J, II:V, 166).

Everyone seeks to be near Julie as part of her immediate community. Saint-Preux complains to Julie that while she is the center of a community, he has no one:

> Yet what a difference from your situation to mine, do please take note! I am not referring to rank and fortune; as to that honor and love must make up for everything. But you are surrounded with people you cherish and who worship you; the attentions of a tender mother, a father whose unique hope is in you; the friendship of a cousin who seems to breathe only through you; a whole family of which you are the ornament; an entire town proud to have known you from birth, everything occupies and shares your sensibility, and what remains for love is but the least part of what is claimed by the rights of blood and friendship. But I, Julie, alas! Wandering and without family, and almost without fatherland, I have no one on earth but you, and love alone stands me in stead of everything. (J, I:XXI, 60)

Despite Saint-Preux's worry that Julie will have nothing left over for him due to all the others who have claims on her heart, we have seen that Julie has plenty of love to give to Saint-Preux. Julie is able to understand her identity in multiple ways: loving an "other" intimately, for her, does not mean that she cannot love her family, her community, or indeed that she cannot be responsible to others that she has not met, or will never even meet. Rousseau shows us that Julie loves *better* than her lover does, and that in loving better she has better judgment. Because she does not maintain an identity as manly citizen of the fatherland who must sacrifice individual ties for the "general will," Julie is able to seek out various perspectives (including those usually not heard), to juggle conflicting opinions, and to contribute to collective decisions that recognize human responsibility for each and all members of community, even those marginalized from the dominant discourse. In her role as mistress of Clarens, Julie convincingly argues *against* many of the prescriptions mandated in *Social Contract*, *The Government of Poland*, and *Letter to D'Alembert*. Julie's constant frustration at her inability to express her passion within the "open" society, her advocacy of public gatherings of the servants where the sexes mix in an "intimate" commerce, her dismay over male control of women, the love and friendship she shares with her cousin Claire, and her willingness to die all point to Rousseau's sympathies with Julie and his unwillingness to fully embrace manliness as a good model for citizenship. We can safely conclude that Emile, Saint-Preux, and Wolmar do not make good citizens. How could they be citizens of a polity required to make good decisions for all when they are so pathetically *unable* to do what is best even for those closest to them? Yet the nagging question remains: Does Rousseau really intend for us to conclude, then, that the women he describes (Sophie, Julie, and Claire) might be models for a better kind of citizen?

What constitutes democratic and participatory citizenship as opposed to passive or tacit citizenship? When we concentrate on Rousseau's women, the dangers of manly citizenship are highlighted. Within the model of manly citizenship, women are completely excluded,[21] while the reason and sentiment of *one man* (with Emile, Saint-Preux, or Wolmar searching for the common in himself to apply as the general will for all) is taken to stand for all men. This common will within men is exemplified in the office of the legislator in the *Social Contract*. Rousseau notes that "in order to discover the rules of society best suited to nations, a superior intelligence beholding all the passions of men without experiencing any of them would be needed" (SC, 214). Though this office "nowhere enters into the Constitution" and "has nothing in common with the human empire" (SC, 214), when we look closely at the gender politics in Rousseau's oeuvre, we clearly see that this superior intelligence is merely the "common" will of all *men*. As I have noted, when we look to Rousseau's sympathetic depiction of women, the text invites an interpretation of Rousseau as unwilling to sacrifice his women (even his men) for this version of passive citizenship inconsistent with principles of justice. In an analysis of Levinas's work on the dangers of reducing diverse and other voices to the same or the common in all, Wendy Farley has argued against the kind of politics exemplified in the standard interpretation of Rousseau's general will:

> The primordial error in Western philosophy is that . . . it reverses the proper roles of particulars and universals: it ontologizes universals and reduces particulars to mere exemplars. . . . With this erasure of the reality of beings in their actual, fragile livingness comes a deafness to their claims to justice. The epistemological primacy of being over beings has as its ethical corollary a trivialization of actually existing creatures: an indifference to their beauty and inoculation against their suffering.[22]

When we read Rousseau from the vantage point of his women characters, this "primordial error" of Western philosophy is not reinscribed. In pointing to the effects that the common will has on women, the marginalized, and the speechless, Rousseau reveals his own dissatisfaction with a society that is *above* politics.

Allowing and encouraging Rousseau's women to speak clearly and forcefully in the words of their own desire would constitute a more active and participatory and, dare I say, *unruly* politics. Bringing passion and desire (exemplified in the feminine) back into the polity would significantly complicate things. As we have seen, none of Rousseau's women are willing to rank various priorities; none are willing to disregard the sometimes unpopular opinions of the marginalized; none are willing to put the good of the whole above the grief of the one; none are willing to count and measure and number items that are clearly incommensurable; none are willing to put a clear and identifiable name on their conflicting identities and passions. The unwillingness of Rousseau's women to reduce the confusing reality of everyday life and decisions of justice to fit an orderly grid is reminiscent of the confusion that Rousseau finds within the city amongst diverse groups of people who simultaneously hold varying opinions, alter their identities, and confront each other in public places. In this milieu one can never really predict, or maybe never even know, what another person is thinking; one is never really sure of another's earnestness, authenticity, devotion to the nation. This tragic loss (though indeed there was *nothing* to lose) of authenticity and identity in modern life so permeates all aspects that one can never even know what one's *lover* is thinking.

Baudelaire beautifully illustrates the loss and possibility inherent in modern sensibility in *The Eyes of the Poor*. In this brief prose poem, the male lover "hates" his beloved for being "the most beautiful example of feminine impermeability anyone can meet."[23] From the man's perspective, Baudelaire writes that "though we had duly promised each other that all our thoughts should be shared in common, and that our two souls henceforth be but one," this turns out to be only a "dream" that although "dreamed by every man on earth . . . has been realized by none."[24] This man's dream is shattered upon realization that he and his lover respond differently to the "eyes of the poor." The man feels ashamed by their own "glasses and decanters, too big for our thirst." He turns his eyes to the woman, hoping "to read *my* thoughts in them." But what he finds there shocks him. The woman also is disturbed by the eyes of the poor, but she comes to a radically different conclusion—she wants to hide from their searching eyes: "Those people are insufferable with their great saucer eyes. Can't you tell the proprietor to send them away?"[25] In Marshall Berman's interpretation of Baudelaire's prose, both responses are equally futile. The man's liberal sentimentality toward the poor is just as empty as the woman's desire to purge the poor from the community. Baudelaire seems to realize that only the most radical reconstruction of modern society could ever begin to heal the personal and social wounds of the exclusion of the marginalized.[26]

It is my contention that Rousseau's ambiguity about his own "solution" of the social contract points toward a similar recognition. In his impulse to heal the wounds created by the inequalities of the Old Regime, Rousseau seems to advocate a fraternal brotherhood based in male will. But when we shift our perspective to the women this fraternity excludes, Rousseau's trust in his own solution begins to quake. There are hints of an alternative, and echoes of Baudelaire's recognition of futility, in a letter written by Saint-Preux concerning Julie's attitude toward the "eyes of the poor":

> She is extremely sensible to ill-being, both hers and others'; and it would not be easier for her to be happy seeing people in misery than for the upright man to preserve his virtue ever pure while keeping constant company with the wicked. She has not that heartless pity that is content to turn away its eyes from ills it could relieve. She goes seeking them out in

order to heal them; it is the existence of unfortunates and not the sight of them that tortures her. (J, V:II, 436)

Through the voice of Saint-Preux, we learn even more about Julie's character and the alternative path her perspective embodies. Though Rousseau is unable to develop a complete solution to the modern dilemmas wrought by the "loss" of identity, authenticity, and transparency, the voices of his women gesture toward a more active and participatory political ideal. This ideal is rooted in private space but extends outward. His women deny the hierarchy between public and private so sacred to Rousseau's men and to the ideal of manly citizenship. Again, Saint-Preux says of Julie:

> She inquires about the needs of her neighborhood with the warmth she puts into her own interests; she knows all its inhabitants; she extends to it, so to speak, her family circle, and spares no care to hold off all the sentiments of suffering and pain to which human life is subjected. (J, V:II, 436)

Punctuated in the excerpt above, it is clear that no matter from which perspective we read Rousseau, the personal and the political are inextricably bound: we learn to be citizens in our most intimate relationships with our families, our friends, our lovers. When we read Rousseau from the perspective of his women, gender boundaries, identity, and authenticity are radically subverted. Saint-Preux articulates the paradox at the heart of Rousseau's texts:

> Julie, ah, what would I have been without you? Cold reason would have enlightened me, perhaps; a tepid admirer of the good, I would at least have loved it in others. I shall do more; I shall know how to practice it with zeal, and imbued with your wise lessons, I shall one day make those who have known us say: Oh what men we all would be, if the world were full of Julies and of hearts that knew how to love them! (J, II:XIII, 188)

Is it the case that Rousseau's women are merely "celestial objects" who inspire men to become manly citizens? Or does a reading of Rousseau's texts from the perspective of his women point elsewhere? These women clearly realize that they *cannot* live in a man's world, that the model of manly citizen excludes them and their feminine desire. The results of this exclusion are clear from the fate of Sophie and Julie.

Rousseau's texts remain the site of critical negotiation concerning the role that women could and should play in society, particularly as potential citizens. As we will see in the chapters that follow, Germaine de Staël saw a potential for a democratic alternative portrayed in the construction of the feminine in Rousseau that others missed. In contrast to the dominant voices of the French Revolution who read in Rousseau a prescription for the suppression of women's citizenship and an edict that all must be the same in order to participate in republican democracy, Staël builds on an alternative in Rousseau to articulate another vision. Informed by those excluded from having a legitimate say in revolutionary politics, Staël takes a lesson from Rousseau in listening to critical voices to assess the present and the future.

4

The Loving Citizen

Staël's Delphine

·

When Germaine de Staël published her novel *Delphine* in 1802, she claimed to have focused her narrative on love in an attempt to avoid writing about politics. Taking the lead from Rousseau's *La Nouvelle Héloïse*, *Delphine* is written in epistolary form. Staël writes in the preface to the novel:

> The letters I have collected were written early in the Revolution; to the extent permitted by the demands of continuity, I have carefully struck from these letters everything that might be related to the political events of those times. (D, Preface:8)

Despite her bold declaration of political distance, Staël intentionally undermines her stance in making a case for the supposed "truth" of the message contained within her fiction:

> I believe that life's circumstances, being ephemeral, teach us less about enduring truths than the fictions based on those truths and that the best lessons of delicacy and self-respect may be found in novels where feelings are portrayed naturally enough for you to believe you are witnessing real life as you read. (D, Preface:5)

And so, Staël tells us a story, the story of *Delphine*. It is a story of an ill-fated love between Delphine (a supporter of the French Revolution) and Léonce (later tried as a traitor by the Revolutionary Tribunal) played out against the backdrop of early events of the Revolution up to the deposition of the King. In *Delphine*, Staël illuminates the wrongs of the Revolution propagated through the silencing of its women. Her story persuades us of the centrality of feeling in political deliberation, the plurality and incommensurability of human goods, the value of love as an epistemology, and the impact of women on political life. Napoleon desperately feared the story's success. In fact, he was so convinced that Staël was *always* writing about politics, even when writing fiction, that he ordered her exile in 1803.[1]

Immersed in building an empire at the time of *Delphine*'s publication, Napoleon had good reason to fear Staël's presence as a novelist, a philosopher, and a political force. Almost every idea in *Delphine* challenges Napoleon's politics. Avriel Goldberger concludes that it is "scarcely surprising that Napoleon treated this book, set ten years earlier, as a covert attack on his regime" (D, Intro:xvii). Early in the revolutionary process, Staël had become disillusioned by the increasingly exclusive constructions of the roles of Woman and citizen. In her *Reflections on the Trial of the Queen, by a Woman*, which she published anonymously in 1793, Staël constructed an impassioned defense of Marie-Antoinette in the belief that the outcome of the queen's trial would affect the destiny of women as a whole in the Revolution.[2] The representation of the queen as the "quintessential unruly woman" had "multiple political ramifications."[3] Most important, Marie-Antoinette's execution signaled a turning point for women in the new republic;[4] after her death, the model of republican motherhood obliterated options for women's participation in politics.[5] Because of the supposed conflicting demands of their nature, women were denied the right of meeting in political associations. After all, the queen had been tried as a "bad mother."

Written at the juncture between the monarchy and the republic, *Delphine* fits neither ideology of Woman. Nevertheless, Staël embraces her identity as a woman as the dominant lens through which she views the Revolution. As such, she undertakes the dangerous move of embracing some of the many stereotypes of Woman promoted by revolutionary republicans and Napoleon—that women are more compassionate, generous, self-sacrificing, and loving—in order to make an argument for women's active citizenship and a transformation of the public sphere based on these transformative moral values. This move is dangerous in that it runs the risk of simply reinforcing the gender roles keeping women out of politics. Moreover, it also fits uncomfortably with women's often violent political action.[6] Yet, Staël sees her feminine nature not as an essential characteristic (she fights conventional norms for women), but rather as a *political* fact that, however dangerous, she must seek to negotiate. In her novels and political theory, Staël confronts the ambiguity of being a woman at a time when political rights were being claimed in terms of the abstract and genderless individual, but granted to men only.[7] Though it was possible for women to demand active citizenship in theory, they were denied these rights in practice.

Examining the Revolution from her perspective as a woman, Staël illuminates what she believes went wrong with Enlightenment ideals as they became embodied in a revolutionary practice that sought to completely exclude women. Staël unremittingly criticizes all the values exhibited by men in the public sphere during the period from the early Revolution to Napoleon's ascent to power. She sharply distinguishes between faults in the various ideologies propagated through the stages of the Revolution, but identifies one important commonality: the Revolution was supposed to create a moral citizen for public life, but had failed miserably in zealously designating that only men should be citizens and in constructing a hyper-masculinist conception of politics. Inspired by Rousseau's disdain for the effeminacy of the aristocracy, the new citizen of France was to be a *real* man. Fashioned after one interpretation of Rousseau, which contained strict rules concerning gender boundaries, the new man/citizen was not to be weakened by feminine sensibilities that were inherently threatening to masculinity.

Seeking to acquire such radical autonomy had its costs. The first was the determination that despite the fact that (or perhaps because) women had understood the revolutionary process to include them and had acted accordingly, after 1793 revolutionary men determined that women could not be citizens. "Women, as 'familial' creatures, and love, as particularized passion, were set opposed irrevocably to political virtue and public duty."[8] But Staël argues that in banishing women from politics, the Revolution lost sight of essential qualities that make good citizens. According to Staël, these qualities are ones that were traditionally associated with the female gender. As we saw in Rousseau's depiction, men do not know how to be proper citizens *because* they do not know how to love and respect others, particularly their women—a connection that Staël sees as crucial. Staël's description of women's morality (their feminine difference) and their potential role in politics supports the conclusion that the exclusion of women from the 1789 Revolution *precluded* the actualization of liberty, equality, and the foundation of a viable republic.

Women, Love, and Politics

In 1800, writing an essay entitled *On Literature in Relation to its Social Institutions*, Staël speaks of the inadequacy of literature that fails to see the connections between the silencing of women, the dismissal of love, and the priorities of a politics that leads to war and tyranny. In her examination of Greek poetry, she concludes that the Greeks knew nothing of ties of love.[9] As Staël notes, "even sons hardly respected their mothers . . . Telemachus orders Penelope to be silent and she leaves imbued with admiration for his wisdom."[10]

When Staël reads Homer's *Odyssey*, she is quick to notice the silencing of Penelope and the power and promise of what Penelope tried to say. She searches, in other words, for a subversive feminine presence; she is attentive to any indication that when women's subjectivity is called into being, it is not immediately foreclosed. Staël looks for the disruptive moment, the possibility of crisis and critique. She is also keen to see the relevance of Homer to France's own dilemma. Throughout the stages of the French Revolution, Staël repeatedly targets "philosophic fanaticism" as one of the evils of the Revolution (CFR, I:I:IV, 58). She links this propensity to disregard concrete situations and reduce irreducible differences to general formulas with the construction of masculinity. In short, men have a propensity to "simplify calculations" due to their lack of sophistication in matters of feeling. Staël argues that "women are the ones at the heart of everything relating to humanity, generosity, delicacy" (OLF, II:II, 204). She argues that during the Terror, men lost their hearts, their ability to feel; it was political dogmas that reigned, not men: "Robespierre had acquired the reputation of high democratical virtue, and was believed incapable of personal views" (CFR, II:III:XIX, 142). Of her first meeting with Napoleon Bonaparte, Staël writes: "I had a vague feeling that no emotion of the heart could act upon him . . . he regards a human being as an action or a thing, not as a fellow creature . . . he does not hate nor does he love" (CFR, II:III:XXVI, 197-198). During Napoleon's reign, "friendship and love . . . were frozen in every heart . . . men no longer cared for one another" (CFR, II:IV:VIII, 306).

In writing the story of *Delphine*, Staël hoped that she could convince France of the travesty in sacrificing personal concerns and love of particular others in the service of power, military glory, and national pride. Staël would agree with Nietzsche's estimation that "all great problems demand *great love*."[11] *Delphine* is her way of illustrating the potential of love as a transformatory political vision. She hoped her story would be a strong critical force that might persuade all to forge a different path, a new way to look at politics, and consider learning to love as central in the education of citizenry.

Delphine and Léonce: Moralities in Conflict

From the outset of the novel, it is apparent that Delphine is out of step with her counterparts in society. As a woman, Delphine rejects the confines of social convention, which are especially strict for women. In their place, she embraces the principles of authenticity, freedom, and the Revolution. Delphine is an aristocratic woman willing to defend liberal notions of freedom. She is considered much too fond and approving of the Revolution, authenticity, and individuality (in the sense of being true to one's self rather than being apparent to all) even in salon society, where such views, *particularly* as expressed by a woman, are unpopular (D, I:2, 13–14).

Madame de Vernon, Delphine's disloyal friend, describes the source of Delphine's charm (the "prettiest and wittiest of women") as the result of an education based exclusively on "philosophy and romantic ideas" encouraged by an "eccentric husband and his deformed sister" (D, I:9, 29–30). By remaining single following her husband's death (exciting "envy" by doing without the "support of a man"), Delphine cultivates her independence and autonomy, charming salon society through her intelligence and wit (D, I:7, 22–25).

Léonce, on the other hand, represents the interests and morality of the Old Regime. His actions are governed by a respect for authority and reverence to duty. He writes to his tutor, M. Barton:

> Although I received an enlightened upbringing, thanks to you, the most
> powerful motives for all the acts of my life are nonetheless a sort of mili-
> tary instinct, prejudices if you will, but the prejudices of my ancestors,
> perfectly suited to the pride and impetuosity of my soul. (D, I:18, 44–47)

Born of a Spanish mother and French father, Léonce is "torn asunder
by two equal forces: a sensitive passionate heart and a proud character
quick to anger" (D, I:18, 46). This tension in his soul is reflected in
Léonce's dilemma in having to choose between love and duty. Though
he is pained by moral decisions, Léonce looks outside himself for answers. He is unwilling to respond to, and many times unwilling even to
consult, his own conscience or inner moral compass. For example, in response to Delphine's request that he resist fighting for the forces of
aristocracy in the battle for power raging in France, Lèonce replies:

> I concede that for myself, I would not make it a point of honor to main-
> tain the privileges of the nobility, but for me it is enough that some of
> the older gentry have decided this is the way things should be, to find in-
> tolerable the idea of being thought a democrat. Even if I were right a
> thousand times over when I explained my position, I do not even want
> an explanation to be necessary in anything related to my respect for my
> ancestors and the duties they have handed down to me. (D, III:32, 243)

Léonce admits that it doesn't matter what he thinks as long as he is
able to decipher the interests and principles of the class in which he is a
member. He says to Delphine: "You love liberty out of generosity" (D,
III: 32, 243) In contrast, he works *against* liberty only out of imposed
duty—a duty he hopes to replicate in his relationship with Delphine
whereby he would not only be "lover" as an equal to Delphine, but
"protector" seeking to "guide" and "admire" her simultaneously (D,
III: 32, 244). In these ways, he is similar to Emile, Saint-Preux, and
Wolmar—who all love their women only as lovable objects rather than
as subjects in their own right.

Staël is insistent in her condemnation of any morality or moral action based on an unquestioned acceptance of social convention, relig-
ious piety, or adherence to the interests of one's class. In portraying a
woman, Delphine, as authentically moral, and a man, Léonce, as weak
and spineless, Staël mocks Rousseau's gendered double standard where-

by men must act authentically and morally, while women obey the dictates of virtue in obeying social convention.[12] Staël argues that *all* citizens, regardless of gender, must be willing to exercise moral judgment that honors commitments to particular others and to community.

Staël's portrayal of Delphine as a moral heroine implies that one must constantly search for disjunctions between the social validity of norms and their hypothetical validity from the standpoint of the standards of justice and moral action.[13] Delphine's constant struggle to determine the morality of her actions (regardless of public opinion) in all complex situations versus Léonce's simplistic following of rules reveals the continual scrutinizing of one's conscience in a contextualization of opposing and incommensurable principles as a key basis for what Staël considers to be authentic and loving moral deliberation. Delphine, in fact, *never* sticks to *any* rules, not even the rules that she makes up for herself. Matilde admonishes Delphine for her belief that "there are no fixed principles on anything"; she asks what virtue would be if "one followed all one's impulses" (D, II: 27, 147).

Delphine's actions reveal that the assumption that there are only two ways to conceptualize moral choice is mistaken; one should not have to choose between unthinking slavery to one's impulses and virtue imposed by duty (here duty might be determined by public opinion, the general will, or even one's inner moral compass). This simplistic opposition between desire and restraint mirrors the formulation of the seemingly perpetual tension between individual and community. The dilemma as posed by the opposition between liberals and communitarians assumes that when we make collective decisions, we must choose between individual desire (or family loyalty or self-interest) and community or general good.[14] Liberals maintain that the general good emerges from individuals following their own self-interest, but here the good is defined in such a limited way as to constitute mere negative freedom. On the other hand, communitarians assume that when we follow our emotions (our impulses, our self-interest, and our loyalty to loved ones or friends), the community, or the general good, suffers. In response to the inability of liberal theory to posit a more developed conception of the good, communitarians argue that we must neglect the self-interest or desire of each in an attempt to mandate the good of all (though how we come to this good is often problematic, as we saw from the dominant interpretation of Rousseau's manly citizens). Staël's work points beyond this impasse in her description of the way Delphine attempts to be loyal to her friends and family without neglecting the general good or denying the need to recognize the claims of others, especially those excluded from the dominant discourse. Delphine's guiding maxim speaks to contextualization, plurality, and situated critical thinking; she seeks to act as "generosity" and "pity" require given the situation (D, I: 29, 74).

At first glance, it may seem that such a standard, as Staël has described it as based loosely on love and defined broadly in terms of generosity and pity, would allow Delphine flexibility to the point of arbitrariness in defining the realm and consequence of moral action. But in fact, she is far from arbitrary or carefree. Delphine (as opposed to the characters in the novel who ascribe to codes of honor, reputation, or virtue) is perpetually engaged in a moral dialogue with herself and others. The abstract code of morality based on honor and reputation calls for adherence to strict yet abstract guidelines that the actor has no part in deciding (eliciting reflex actions from Léonce). Delphine accuses Léonce of following a morality "based on honor alone" (D, III: 14, 217). In contrast, Delphine's concrete and contextualized code calls on her to act on loving commitments to both friends and humanity. This requires a constant engagement from the actor in the ongoing confrontation with various moral dilemmas. One of strongest objections Delphine has to the way that Léonce makes decisions is that the rules he follows are rigid and inflexible. Delphine's actions imply that she harbors a deep suspicion of any attempt to create an order out of social life that institutes a set of rules unresponsive to dialogue and debate.

An example from *Delphine* will serve to illustrate the specific contours of the kind of moral engagement that Staël's heroine brings to every situation and that by implication, would be demanded of the just citizen. Possibly the most important moment in the narrative is the first time Delphine self-consciously opts to act in a morally responsible and authentic way to a friend, knowing that the consequence of her action may be Léonce's scorn and disapproval (D, I:22–38, 53–94). After Delphine has discovered (much to her chagrin) that she loves Léonce, though he is promised to another, she is forced into a moral quandary over her friend Thérèse's illicit love affair. Thérèse is mother to a nine-year-old girl, Isore, born of a loveless, imposed marriage to a much older and ill-deserving man, M. d'Ervins, who makes her life miserable. By chance, Thérèse meets and falls in love with M. de Serbellane, and the two begin an affair.

A series of events unfolds to reveal the illicit affair, and Thérèse finds herself threatened by her husband and incapable of protecting her daughter. Delphine is caught in the unfortunate position of being asked to fulfill a promise to her friend in agreeing to arrange one last meeting between Thérèse and her lover in her home. Delphine knows, however, that arranging this meeting (implicitly condoning the illicit affair) will fly in the face of social convention and displease and embarrass Léonce. She hesitates to fulfill her promise, knowing that the results will be her own chastisement and the possible loss of Lèonce's love. She laments:

> Must I admit the feeling that gave me pause? If by some chance, Lèonce discovers that I have brought together in my home a married woman and her lover against her husband's express orders, will he approve of me? . . . Am I no longer capable of judging for myself what generosity and pity may require of me? (D, I:29,73–74)

After a long struggle with herself in which Delphine examines the demands of social norms for women, the way that Léonce sees the world, and her own understanding of what "pity" and "generosity" require, Delphine decides to act on her loyalty to her friend Thérèse.

It is important to note that Delphine's actions constitute a betrayal of her own self-interest as well as the conventional norms of abstract duty. Note also that Delphine's actions are reminiscent of those of Rousseau's Claire who judges Julie by the standards of friendship rather than of self-interest, virtue, or duty. Staël's portrayal of the way Delphine agonizes over this decision in her consideration of her reputation in the eyes of Léonce, the demands of conventional society, and the norms of justice (as she defines them) points beyond the choice between self-interest and duty. In making her decision, the most important step in the process is Delphine's consideration of Thérèse's dilemma. In Delphine's mind, in order to be a loyal friend (and a just citizen) she must carefully consider the concrete particularity of Thérèse's desire and situation. To come to a decision that would conform to the demands of justice, Delphine must consider Thérèse as a single and irreplaceable person, someone to whom she owes loyalty as a friend. We will see later how Staël demonstrates the concern for particular others when that other is a stranger.

The result of the meeting between Thérèse and her lover in Delphine's home is, as expected, disastrous for Delphine's personal life. The lovers are discovered; the husband and lover promise to duel over Thérèse's honor; Delphine trusts her so-called friend Madame de Vernon (mother of Matilde, the woman Léonce is meant to marry) to plead her case to Léonce; Madame de Vernon leads Léonce to draw his own conclusions about what M. de Serbellane was doing in Delphine's home late at night; and Léonce decides to marry Matilde, convinced that Delphine has irrevocably wronged him. Part One of *Delphine* ends with Léonce married to Matilde, and Delphine a social outcast because of her generosity in accepting the blame for the duel so as not to put Thérèse in danger of losing her daughter.

Love's Political Message

Delphine's and Léonce's mutual attraction is, to say the least, rather disconcerting for the reader. Even Delphine recognizes the "astonishing contrast of [their] characters" (D, I:19, 47). Léonce represents all that Delphine will fight long and hard against—the hierarchy of political honor over love, an inability to act on feelings, and an uncritical acceptance of public opinion. Indeed, *appearances* are everything to Léonce. In this sense, Léonce is a typical Rousseauian antihero. Tracy Strong argues that the scandal of politics for Rousseau consists of a "situation where each individual lives, as it were, outside him- or herself."[15] Rousseau's account of the *worst* citizen is as follows:

> The citizen, always active, sweats, scurries, constantly agonizes in search of still more strenuous occupations: he works to his death, even rushes towards it in order to be in a position to live. . . . The sociable man, always outside himself, only knows how to live in the opinion of others, and, so to speak, derives the sentiment of his own existence solely from their judgment (DI, 115).

Strong argues that for Rousseau "'true philosophy' consists in 'returning into oneself and listening to the voice of conscience.'"[16] This is precisely what Lèonce proves unable to do. In making some inquiries about the man who is to become her cousin Matilde's husband, Delphine hears from an acquaintance of his that though Léonce is quite witty, he is "extravagantly obsessed with what he calls reputation or public opinion, and ready to sacrifice the primary interests of life for even the shadow of that opinion" (D, I:10, 31).

In a bold affront to dominant interpretations of Rousseau's sexual politics, Staël imbues Delphine's character with behaviors that Rousseau finds to be crucial for *men*, though democratically refashioned in her women. Delphine is described by Staël as possessing a "remarkable mind," demonstrating "singularly independent" opinions in her disregard for "society's arbitrary conventions" (D, I: 2–3, 13–17). Because she is a woman, though, these qualities are Delphine's burden.[17] Though her heroine is "charming," even "brilliant," Staël recognizes that she will have great difficulty in pursuing the love of her dreams. No "prudent man would be eager to wed a person who sees everything by her own lights, acts according to her own ideas, and often disregards time-honored precepts."[18]

Oddly enough, Delphine's and Léonce's differing characters seem to mesh. When Delphine meets Léonce, she notes "so much sweetness and sensibility written on his face . . . that [she] entirely forgot the opinion [she] had of him that might have protected [her] heart" (D, I: 20, 50). Léonce, for his part, recognizes Delphine's independent ways even at their first meeting, but observes optimistically that "superior intelligence and a *timid character* are *both* portrayed in her gaze . . . she combines an independent mind with a devoted heart *easily subjugated* when she loves" (D, I: 21,52, emphasis added). The accounts by Delphine and Léonce of their first meeting reveal the extent to which their attraction is based on a supreme and tragic mutual misunderstanding. Delphine thinks that Léonce's sensitivity outweighs his respect for duty and honor as constructed in social opinion. Léonce thinks that Delphine's independent spirit would easily submit to love of a man. Both parties turn out to be quite wrong in their initial judgments.

The heart of the misunderstanding lies in their differing conceptions of the nature of love and the question of whether love, in itself, fosters bonds of illegitimate dependency. Lèonce understands love as a purely private emotion, subject to sacrifice, if necessary, in the quest for higher political or social goals. Thus, though Léonce lacks the integrity of conscience that Rousseau's Emile displays, he has fully internalized Rousseau's lesson that one must seek to control one's passions in the face of political decisions.

As we learned in Chapter 2, Emile reports to his beloved Sophie that the "rights of humanity" (however defined) are "more sacred" to him than Sophie's needs, clearly ranking in order what he considers to be his conflicting duties (E, V:441). Likewise, Léonce is certain that his love for Delphine will get in the way of his political convictions. In a world characterized by opposition between private emotion and public sacrifice, the public must always take precedence for men, and the private must always take precedence for women. It follows, then, that Léonce would necessarily feel certain that Delphine's independent spirit could be sacrificed to love of a man, whereas his own love for Delphine must never interfere with his preconceived ideals of political duty.

Staël challenges these boundaries and their accompanying sexual politics. In her *Considerations on the Principal Events of the French Revolution*, Staël notes that the king of France and all those who perished at the guillotine were capable of private virtue but *unable to extend* that virtue to political affairs.[19] In contrast, Staël's heroine Delphine understands love as *intimately connected to politics*, a feeling born of passion for another human being and humanity *at one and the same time*. Staël is clearly convinced that love is a morally relevant way to know the world and that this knowledge of how to love has an appropriate place in political discussions. In her defense of Marie-Antoinette, for example, Staël makes an emotional appeal to the "hearts of women of all classes and from every nation."[20] She claims that the queen could never have committed the crimes of which she was accused, crimes of treason and the persecution of the French people, for she has a "woman's heart." Staël hinges her defense of the queen on her devotion to the king and her children, evidence of her *ability to love*, claiming that "whoever knows how to love, could never cause suffering" (Q, 376). For Staël, if one knows how to love privately with passion and commitment, one should bring these talents to the public sphere as a good citizen. Staël argues that her father's greatness as a statesman lay in his inability to separate the love that his wife felt for him (so "sincere and impassioned") from "any circumstance in his life," including his addresses to the Assembly (CFR, I:II:XVIII, 390). Staël asserts that "he who is capable of true and profound emotion is never intoxicated by power; and it is by this, *above all,* that we recognize in a minister true greatness of soul" (CFR, I:II:XVIII, 390, emphasis added).

Though Léonce *says* he loves Delphine, his obsession with reputation will lead him to doubt Delphine's judgments and actions as an independent woman. As readers, we want Delphine and Léonce to consummate their love, but we also resent the pressure Léonce puts on Delphine to become someone she is not in order to *merit* his love. The love Léonce expects and requires of Delphine is a love that insists that Delphine cease being who she is—an independent woman—to become the *wife* of Léonce. The kind of love that Staël articulates in portraying Delphine as a loving *citizen* and *friend* is a love that transgresses the boundary between private and public in becoming *political.* As such, Staël promotes love (emotion/passion) as an epistemology that is valuable for political life. This kind of love is appropriate as a measure for political action and for moral deliberation of public affairs.

Joan Tronto notes that within the debates of feminist theorists, the ethic of care has been labeled by some as a specifically "woman's morality." Tronto finds this to be politically dangerous for women, given that historically the image of moral women "often excluded women of color, immigrant women, poor women, lesbians, and women who were not 'fit' mothers."[21] Such feminist arguments, thus, end up excluding those who are powerless. The claim for a superior women's morality also reinforces the Rousseauian idea articulated in *Emile, or On Education* that men and women are essentially different and "these relations and these differences must have a moral influence" (E, V:358). Yet, though Staël appeals to the feminine, even to the "hearts of women," her work is not so easily classified as essentialist. Her use of love is strategic, rather than essential, and it always carries with it an epistemological and political function.

To illustrate the connections between love and politics and explain how these connections might be interpreted as calling into being a new conception of justice and citizenship, let me return to the example of Staël's defense of Marie-Antoinette. In thinking about why and how Staël appeals to the hearts of women to defend Marie-Antoinette, it is important to remember that Marie-Antoinette was vilified on the grounds of her identity as Woman (especially in her violation of Woman's place by being a political woman) and Outsider (as Austrian and not French). Lynn Hunt argues that the crimes Marie-Antoinette was said to have committed can be traced back to her status as a dangerous woman: "Promiscuity, incest, poisoning of the heir to the throne, plots to replace the heir with a pliable substitute—all of these charges reflect a fundamental anxiety about queenship as the most extreme form of women invading the public sphere."[22]

Marie-Antoinette was seen to have "invaded" the public sphere because she was both a woman and a foreigner: she fundamentally did not belong, did not speak the same language of politics. These are the important aspects of her identity that Staël plays with in her defense. Staël says that rather than accuse the queen of treason for her ties with her Austrian family, we should see her as virtuous: "[H]er entire life has been proof of her respect for the ties of nature—but this virtue, far from frightening us, should set our minds at ease about all of the others" (Q, 373). Moreover, according to Staël, in any acts she has done, she has only been motivated by a love for her family:

> You, who saw her look at her children, you who know that no danger
> could reconcile her to being separated from her spouse, even when so
> many times he left paths open for her to return to her country—can you
> believe that her heart was barbarous or tyrannical? Ah! no one who
> knows what it is to love would make others suffer; perhaps no one who
> has been punished through those whom one cherishes could doubt celestial vengeance (Q, 377).

Staël lists further proof against the charges that Marie-Antoinette was a bad mother and a traitor to the nation. The only time, according to Staël, that the queen lost her composure or acted out of anything even approaching self-interest was when one of her family members was in danger. "If you want to weaken a grand character," Staël writes, "arrest her children" (Q, 379). According to Staël's account, when Marie-Antoinette was separated from her son, he refused to "take the slightest nourishment" (Q, 390). For Staël, the son's determination testifies to the mother's character: "Judge for yourself the kind of mother who has already succeeded in inspiring such an energetic and profound feeling at such a tender age!" (Q, 390). Staël claims Marie-Antoinette lived only for and through her children: "[S]he remains alive because she loves, because she is a mother: ah, but for this sacred bond, she would excuse herself from the company of those who want to prolong her life" (Q, 391).

Unfortunately, the only ones who wanted to prolong the queen's life were doing so in order to place her at the guillotine for being a bad woman and mother. Anne Mini insightfully notes that Staël's defense of the queen hinges on an account of how her roles as Woman suddenly "crashed into one another—roles over which the young queen had even less control than most women."[23] Astonishingly, Marie-Antoinette did not step out of the prescribed social roles for women, but was still condemned as a bad Woman and mother. Staël's brilliant insight lies in her recognition that it was the queen's marginal status as woman and foreigner that were her condemning traits in the eyes of the revolutionaries. Staël takes the leap of bringing emotion and family ties into the realm of public politics in order to show that by the revolutionaries' own criteria, the queen was indeed a good mother. Moreover, in urging a recognition of the life of the wife of the king, daughter of Maria-Theresa, a foreigner, Staël inches us toward a conception of justice wherein the recognition of, and listening to, others and outsiders is key.

The recognition of others, even if strangers, is best learned through a deep and lasting connection to and care for particular others in our lives. When we have learned to love another, we can learn to extend those feelings of respect and care to a person that we have never met. This is not to say that we must "love" or even *like* strangers who have no immediate connection to us. It is also not to say that as a democratic and plural community, we must equally acknowledge and tolerate all versions of the good or be paralyzed by a recognition of the singularity of persons. Wendy Farley aptly states:

> It should be evident that discourse and society should be opened up to women, lesbians and gay men, people of color. It should be equally ev-

ident that society should not be opened up to child-torturers, serial killers, or rapists.[24]

That said, we must recognize that in considering every person as single and irreplaceable, someone whose absence would profoundly affect a number of other people to whom that person is attached, we must still proceed to make just decisions in terms of community good. Yet that vision of the community good or the procedures that are meant to ensure it should never be fixed or impermeable. When we try to permanently fix social arrangements, forever determine the general good, and instill order on an ever-changing social situation, the voices of the other and the excluded become inaudible. It is important to recognize that when we consider connections and attachments in the lives of concrete others, it is less easy to defend stable or timeless systems of laws or procedures that systematically end up excluding certain persons.

Moreover, when we allow our commitments to particular others to influence our rational, political judgment, we achieve a richer conception of human and common good. My interpretation of Staël challenges the entire thrust of Kantian and neo-Kantian (Rawlsian) theories of deliberative justice in proposing that a viable human conception of rational self-interest and duty to community is integrally connected to the happiness of particular others. Likewise, Staël asserts that individual happiness, as tied to the good of others, inspires community spirit. As such, our loving ties to others have a primary place in politics, allowing us to envision the good in ways obscured by purely rational and detached deliberation (if, indeed, such deliberation is possible).

Thus in my reading, Staël maintains that a good citizen will consider each person's specific individuality *as well as* general humanity in debating moral questions. Unlike the Rousseau of the *Social Contract* who claims that law should always consider subjects "en masse and actions in the abstract, and never a particular person or action" (SC, II:6, 211), Staël warns against the danger of correcting diversities of opinion "like faults in discipline"(CFR, II:IV:II, 241). Staël's conception of morality based on love demands that the good citizen confront moral dilemmas with full knowledge of all relevant facts and concrete information about all individuals concerned. This model of moral deliberation is in direct conflict with models of liberal procedure (roughly speaking, the Girondin model in the eighteenth century and the Rawlsian model in the twentieth[25]), the Rousseauian model of the general will (as Carol Blum argues is represented by Robespierre and radical republicans[26]) and the militaristic model of honor exemplified during Napoleon's empire.

Staël's critique outlines a new vision of citizenship based on the depiction of feminine values historically associated with the aristocracy but now democratically refashioned. In accord with the way Staël connects love and politics, learning to love with passion, compassion, generosity, and sympathy (something that women are taught to do) is the superior education for citizenry. It is important to note that for Staël, conflict is not excluded from what it means to love as a citizen. In fact, as we will see from Staël's models of political deliberation, including passion in the public sphere serves not to displace politics (as Bonnie Honig warns against[27]), but rather dislodges it from an excessively rationalistic and detached form that is highly vulnerable to usurpation by dogmatic idealism. In contrast, Staël creates the portrait of a loving citizen, one who, as an embodied subject, is able to be particularly attentive to the individuality and special needs of others while not losing sight of their attributes as Kantian noumenal selves, equal to all others in rational capacity.[28] This citizen (as a model for reconstructing revolutionary identity) views "each and every rational being as an individual with a concrete history, identity and affective-emotional constitution."[29]

Political Judgments Beyond Objectivity

In the very last scenes of *Delphine,* Staël offers one very clear example of how love might be an appropriate component in making political judgments. In a desperate mood following Léonce's marriage to Matilde, Delphine commits herself to a convent. Shortly thereafter, Matilde dies in childbirth and Léonce is free to pursue Delphine as his wife. But once Léonce discovers that Delphine has committed herself to life as a nun in a convent, both are emotionally distraught. Their mutual friend, M. de Lebensei, suggests a plan. He asks them to remember that France has abolished all monastic laws. He begs them to come to France, to live together as a married couple without guilt, within the law (D, VI:12,

429). M. de Lebensei is convinced that if they do not accept this plan, Delphine and Léonce will die of broken hearts.

As readers, we naively let our hopes rise in anticipation that our ill-fated couple will finally get together. We should know better by now. Léonce is morally incapable of real emotional reciprocity or sacrifice for love. No matter how much M. de Lebensei tries to convince him that Delphine's vows should be disregarded, legally and morally, because the Supreme Being "doubtless knows our nature too well ever to accept irrevocable commitments," (D, VI: 12, 432) Léonce cannot be persuaded. M. de Lebensei asks whether Léonce would forgo the "most beautiful of destinies—love within marriage—because there do exist a few men who will blame [him]" (D, VI: 12, 433). It turns out that Léonce will risk everything for the sake of honor. He remains firm in the convictions he has held all his life: "Life cannot be endured without honor! And human judgments mete out honor: they must be escaped in the grave!" (D, VI: 17, 439). Though Léonce reluctantly agrees to M. de Lebensei's plan, convinced that it is the only way to save Delphine's life, Delphine is unwilling to marry him when he considers it a sacrifice: "Could I accept his hand if he felt it was a sacrifice to give it? His character has separated us before; if it must divide us again, let there be no turning back!" (D, VI: 15, 438).

The only thought that comforts Léonce is engagement in combat. In the midst of their personal struggle, Delphine and Léonce hear of the massacres in Paris. It is September 1792. Léonce recounts his excitement at the thought of leaving Delphine and this personal mess behind to fight gloriously for his class interests:

> In combat, the risks will be mine, and when I choose, I will know how to expose my head to them. No, only in the midst of war could I bear the grief of leaving you; death is always easy there, always present, helping you endure a few last days of life devoted to glory. There my acts will assuage even despair: the blood that must be shed, the danger threatening you, the horror all around, and all the screams of hate which suspend the pains of love for a time. So long as the sword is raised against me, I shall be all right; I shall be better still when it has pierced me to the heart. (D, VI: 18, 442)

In dreaming of combat, Léonce has a fantasy of control, order, and glory. He feels out of control in the realm of love, lost in the battle between his heart and his deference for social opinion. He chooses what he ironically considers the safer, cleaner, more honorable route: war. He says the risks will be *his*; he will *choose* them; the evils of war are necessary and honorable evils; the threat of death will give purpose to his life.

For Staël, Léonce's thinking is typically masculine. To glorify the risks of battle and define honor as dying for one's "duty" requires a method of abstracting from ties to family members, friends, and fellow and sister human beings that does not come easily to the citizen whose knowledge is grounded by loving ties. When writing of Napoleon, Staël most deplores his machismo nature. She notes that "violence suits despotism alone; and accordingly, it showed itself at last under its true name—that of a military chief [Napoleon]: To this the tyrannical measures of the Directory were a prelude" (CFR, II:III: XXVIII, 216).

Staël gives Delphine a glorious last scene in which to display her alternative morality. Léonce goes off, fights honorably defending a fellow aristocrat, but is captured by the defenders of the Revolution at Verdun. He is set to be sentenced to death by the Tribunal when Delphine, in a desperate last attempt to save him, goes to speak to the president of the Tribunal. When she goes to his house, asking to speak to him in private, he responds that "there will be no room for mystery in the life of a public man" (D, Conclusion, 448). Delphine replies that it is she who has secrets and wishes to confide them to him. Her plan is to argue that Léonce had not officially signed up for the counterrevolutionary forces; he was in the wrong place at the wrong time and simply acted honorably in saving another man's life. Everything about the judge indicated that he was an "inflexible" man, yet on her way to talk to him privately, Delphine had noticed "on his desk the portrait of a woman with a child in her arms, and that picture telling her that he was husband and father, momentarily gave her the hope of moving him" (D, Conclusion, 449). Delphine pleads to the judge:

> I [have] proved to you that he [Léonce] had not taken up arms, that he was not your enemy, that he was prompted only by *generosity*, by *friend-*

ship; and even if it were true that your opinions did not coincide with his on the present war, was it not *chance* that threw the best and most sensitive of beings into a different party from yours? Men are alike as *fathers*, as *friends*, but partisan fury can excite only short-lived hatred; hatred that one can feel against powerful enemies but that is instantly snuffed out when they are vanquished, when they are brought down by fate and you see in them only their *private virtues*, their feelings, their misfortune. . . . "Young woman," said the judge, "you insult me because I mean to obey the laws of my country." "You do not know what you ask of me; you are unaware of the risks I would run if I tried to shield M. de Mondoville from the natural course of the law. I would certainly have wished that freedom could be established in France without the death of one man for a political opinion; but in the face of the violent ferment stirred up by this foreign war, do not insist that a family man, forced to accept a painful but necessary post in these difficult times, do not insist that he compromise his own life to save a stranger." . . . "A stranger!" replied Delphine, "if he is innocent! A stranger, if his life depends on you! The unfortunate man we can save from an unjust and certain death *should be so dear to us*! Yes, I agree, what I ask of you requires courage, generosity, sacrifice. It is not ordinary pity I expect of you, it is nobility of soul that supposes the virtues of antiquity, republican virtues, virtues which bring a thousand times more honor to the party you champion than the most illustrious victories." (D, Conclusion, 449-451, emphasis added)

The way Delphine argues Léonce's case subverts the norms of morality imposed by public virtue. She asks that the judge consider Lèonce as a concrete and singular individual, lovingly tied to friends and family. As such, she asks that the kinds of bonds we usually consider as "private" be brought into the public forum in order not to risk harming individuals in the quest for political goals. In the excerpt above, the judge says that he certainly "wished that freedom could be established in France without the death of one man for a political opinion," but he seems to throw up his hands in anguish against the pressures on the Revolution by a "foreign war." It is this logic that Staël has Delphine argue against in bringing emotions into the public forum as a guard against imposing community on individuals.

Note that this method of protecting against totalitarian politics seems to be in sharp contrast to the warnings of Hannah Arendt, who warned *against* bringing emotions into politics. Indeed, in *On Revolution*, Arendt cites this practice as one that led to the Terror. She claims that emotion serves to do the opposite of what Staël predicts; rather than protect particular individuals, individuals are lost in emotion's wake:

> Since the days of the French Revolution, it has been the boundlessness of their sentiments that made revolutionaries so curiously insensitive to reality in general and to the reality of persons in particular, whom they felt no compunctions in sacrificing to their "principles," or to the course of history, or to the cause of revolution as such. While this emotion-laden insensitivity to reality was quite conspicuous already in Rousseau's own behavior, his fantastic irresponsibility and unreliability, it became a political factor of importance only with Robespierre, who introduced it into the factional strife of the Revolution.[30]

Arendt and Staël desire the same result in that both fear the kind of politics that obscures the lives of particular persons, the anguish of particular and localized suffering. Yet though both warn against the muffling of critical voices, Arendt fears that emotion fuels the rush to total certainty (especially as compassion for particular individuals is transformed into pity for the undifferentiated masses), whereas Staël warns against a faith in abstract "reason" and "objective" truth. If we interpret these differences as a choice between a fear of unthinking emotion and the fear of an unfeeling reason, we would simply reinscribe the tensions I have been working to avoid. In searching for a way beyond this version of the impasse, we must recognize that no "reason" is without emotion and likewise that no emotion is pure instinct. Staël's plea to the judge helps us to work toward a way to make decisions as just citizens in a world characterized by deep divisions and plurality. Staël does not ask us to have pity on all defendants or on all people just by virtue of their connections to others. It is "not ordinary pity" that Delphine requires of the judge. She does not ask that the judge simply pity Lèonce, nor does she ask him to identify with him solely as a victim—these kinds of emotions could lead to a faceless politics that wipes out individual identity. Staël asks for something else. She merges the general and the particular in her bid for the judge to see Lèonce as an unfortunate stranger whose life depends on him. What Delphine proposes in this passage is a model whereby citizens practice something akin to what Benhabib has called "enlarged thought." According to Benhabib, this model does not call for

> emotionally assuming or accepting the point of view of the other. It means merely making present to oneself what the perspectives of others involved are or could be, and whether I could "woo their consent" in acting the way I do. . . . To "think from the perspective of everyone else" is to know "how to listen" to what the other is saying, or when the voices of others are absent, to imagine to oneself a conversation with the other as my dialogue partner.[31]

In pressing the judge to think according to the model of enlarged thought, Delphine asks the judge to consider Léonce as a fellow human being, in all his private and personal attributes, his likeness and difference from himself. She asks him to put aside partisan hatred, honor imposed by competing positions in the war over France. She asks him not to *transcend* humanity in his quest for general principles and rules, but rather to consider humanity in its richness and concreteness in defying those general rules. Delphine's quest for a morality appropriate to the public sphere does not factor out private emotions. The judge is asked by Delphine to act in terms of *feelings*, considering *misfortune*, bringing those feelings to bear on the general principles. The laws of the country are only applicable if the judge is able to carry out the sentence in light of Léonce's *concrete humanity.*

Staël's emphasis on concrete humanity raises a host of questions concerning the relationship between particular individuals and abstract philosophy, passionate commitment and general responsibility. Can the truth that Staël tells in *Delphine* be reconciled with the truths of philosophy? What part does love, a commitment to certain and identifiable others, play in determining reason, a quest to treat all as abstract rights-bearing individuals subject equally to higher principles without regard to circumstance? Staël suggests that the oppositions between passion and reason are drawn too boldly. The judge himself admits to the "violent ferment" embodied within the supposedly reasonable laws enacted by the Revolutionary Tribunal. These laws themselves represent only one of the "languages of politics."[32] As J. Peter Euben notes:

> Political wisdom . . . cannot be singular and monological or set in a dis-
> course of command and obedience appropriate to an army but is, rather,
> plural and multiple . . . political knowledge comes from yielding to other
> voices and positions, sharing public space with them rather than con-
> signing them to shadows and whispers . . . or caves and houses.[33]

The truth Staël tells is in part a recognition that we cannot seal off the
complexities of the world, especially in a political forum like a court-
room, under the pretense of making choices—choices that directly affect human good, are commensurable, and are able to be decided simply
and clearly. The fact that human goods are incommensurable, that
choices are difficult, and that to make these choices we must draw on
reason *as informed by passion* is the very stuff of politics. Part of Staël's
brilliance is her warning to students of philosophy and politics that our
reason is always born of some passion and that no matter how hard we
try, we cannot separate ourselves from the ones we love and the ideas
we hold dear.

When the judge begs Delphine to consider *his* private life and not to
ask such a sacrifice for a stranger from a family man, Delphine again
alters the terms of the debate. She insists that Léonce is *not* a stranger to
the judge, once he has knowledge of their common humanity. If the
judge refuses to act on this basis, insisting on humanity's transcendence,
the particularities of humanity will be lost in wars fought over abstract
rules. In order for the sentence to be moral, the judge must have full
knowledge of all the circumstances surrounding Léonce's crime and all
the private aspects of Léonce's life. The judge tries desperately to resist
Delphine's pleas:

> Astonished by his own reaction, the judge put his hands over his eyes so
> that he would not see Delphine, and rediscovering deep in his soul the
> fear that emotion fought, he made one last effort to stifle his pity and cat-
> egorically refused what Madame d'Albemar believed she was about to
> obtain. (D, Conclusion, 451)

What pushes the judge over the edge in submitting to Delphine's
requests is his concern and emotion for his *own* son. Just as the judge refuses, his wife enters the chambers and requests that he come upstairs to
check on their sick son. Delphine seizes on the judge's display of emo-

tion upon hearing of his child's illness, and she predicts that the judge's son will die if the judge sets his "face against pity." Staël recounts:

> At those words, without speaking, the judge's wife pleaded with her husband for Léonce's pardon with her eyes, with her raised arms, almost without realizing what she did. Looking at his wife and Delphine in turn, the judge said: "No, I will refuse nothing so long as my son is in danger; no, whatever may happen to me, Madame, you have won," and taking his pen he wrote the order to free M. de Mondoville. (D, Conclusion, 452)

Emotional blackmail, you say? The judge reconsiders *only* after Delphine appeals to his own familial ties by invoking the love the judge feels for his own son. As long as he remains on the level of intellect and argument, he remains self-confident, entirely unconvinced of the rightness of Delphine's cause. Only when he considers what it would feel like to lose his own son, does he feel a sudden rush of regret that forces him to see the world in a way in which he was previously unable to see it. Using this particular example, Staël aptly demonstrates that it is one thing to ask about one's feelings for family, quite another to be confronted with the possible loss of a particular other that you love.

But the question remains: is the model of political and ethical deliberation advanced here, one that would bring affective relations of the family into the public domain of justice, an unalloyed good? In response to this question, it is important to keep in mind the logic that motivates Staël's requirement that we continually remember our ties to the ones we love. She claims the urgency of this type of emotion, or "learning to love" as I've been calling it, as a way to keep at the front of our minds what is most particular as well as what is more general about our lives as human beings: we are *plural individuals with strong attachments to others.* When we remember this about ourselves—in other words, when we know how to love and how to use that knowledge of how to love in our politics—we are less able to shut out critical or unwelcome voices, less likely to adhere to strict and unchanging rules or to a fixed version of the common good, and more able to make decent decisions as just citizens.

Staël tells us a truth through the narrative of *Delphine,* culminating in the confrontation with the judge, a truth that is part and parcel of political life. Within Staël's text, this truth holds sway. The judge is con-vinced by Delphine's speech and signs an order to release Léonce. Just as this order is being carried out, however, the Tribunal returns and the reprieve is revoked. Léonce is led to his death to be carried out by shooting, Delphine swallows poison on the way, and they die almost si-multaneously. Thus Delphine dies as she lived: publicly, passionately, politically engaged to the end. In congruence with what I argue is Staël's model of *moral* citizenship, Delphine demands sincerity, empa-thy and engagement from her own conscience, her lover, and the judge. Delphine's death is powerfully *political*; she dies as a *loving citizen*.

Private Ethics, Public Virtue

Staël's sensitivity to female subjectivity has particular historical signifi-cance during the transformatory period of the French Revolution. In *Delphine*, Staël focuses largely on interactions in the private sphere, as-suming that the novel contains valuable political lessons. In her *Essay on Fictions* she writes:

> The greatest power of fiction is its talent to touch us; almost all moral truths can be made tangible if they are shown in action. Virtue has so much influence on human happiness or misery that one can make most of life's situations depend on it. Some severe philosophers condemn all emotions, wanting moral authority to rule by a simple statement of moral duty. Nothing is less suited to human nature. (EF, 74)

Staël was not alone in seizing on private morality as the key to a larger public virtue. Ideas of virtue and morality figured prominently in both the private writings and the public discourse of revolutionary fig-ures such as Robespierre and Saint-Just. The idea revitalized in the writings of Rousseau that one must create a *moral citizen* before forming a virtuous society is as old as Socrates. In documenting the impact of Rousseau's work on revolutionary ideals and goals, scholars have noted that the link between private morality and public virtue created "unsta-ble boundaries"[34] between private and public life. Revolutionary leaders claimed that "to be truly Republican, each citizen must expe-rience and bring about in himself a revolution equal to the one that has changed France."[35] According to Robespierre in February 1794, "in the system of the French Revolution, what is immoral is impolitic, what is corrupting is counterrevolutionary."[36]

The French Revolution clearly marked a critical moment for women. After the Revolution, all things were possible. Men were presumably transforming themselves to become citizens of the New France, and women sought to transform themselves along with them. In the blurred boundaries between private and public, all acts were political, all values subject to change. Yet what women like Staël came to discover was that for women to transform themselves from private beings, mothers, and wives into citizens was seen by men as a subversion of the sexual order. As the Revolution gained momentum and became increasingly imbued with violence and terror, the threat to public order was swiftly redefined as a breakdown of sexual roles.[37]

Even dress was politically invested. When women began to don the red liberty cap and form women's clubs, a deputy of the Revolution, Fabre d'Eglantine, denounced the acts as a subversion of the natural order in which women have exclusively familial identities.[38] Seen as at stake when women wore the cockade or the *bonnet rouge* was "the unmanning of revolutionary men."[39] Virtuous, moral behavior for a woman was being constructed in a domestic fashion increasingly dictated by women's *bodies*. In the creation of moral citizens for the New France, women were to be only *private* beings.

In the quest to make moral citizens, Staël adds two powerful insights. First, she proposes that most men are like Léonce or Thérèse's husband: though they try, they don't really know how to love. Men's lack of moral education in this personal sphere leads to political disaster. Léonce, an aristocratic man, represents a look backward to the Old Regime when women had a life outside the home (as in the salon). Delphine's attraction to an aristocrat, Léonce, signifies Staël's own longing for women's past political influence and her ambivalence about the direction that the Revolution takes toward violence and terror. On the other hand, though *revolutionary* men are apt to advance a *private* and familial role for women, they do exhibit democratic political values. But they, as well, are confined by a peculiarly male mentality. Though revolutionary men *espouse* revolutionary values, their transformation does not begin with themselves. In short, *all* men must learn to love, and to love democratically, before the Revolution can have a fighting chance. Control and domination in the private sphere leads directly to the Terror.

Staël's second insight is that to seek a new, more humane direction for the Revolution, we must look to women. Historically, women are the ones who have learned how to love. In order to advance a morality that potentially could transform the reigning social (public) values, we must tap into this epistemology. Staël wished to *unman* revolutionary men in recreating the Revolution in terms of feminine values.[40]

Staël Sketches an Alternative
to the *Social Contract*

Staël's model of the loving citizen is a viable alternative to Rousseau's social contract that builds directly on the alternative model of citizenship I discerned by carefully studying Rousseau's women. To accord with the dictates of Rousseau's social contract, citizens are asked to make a number of "advantageous" exchanges: a "precarious way of living for one that is more secure," "natural independence for liberty," the "power to harm others for security for themselves," and "strength for right" (SC, II:4, 207). In previous chapters, I argued that Rousseau's women refuse to accept the terms of this contract. They display an alternative model for citizenship that integrates individual passions and goods with the larger good of the whole. Staël also rejects the terms of the social contract and builds on the alternative displayed in Rousseau's women by implying that any such "advantageous exchange" required by the social contract is poised to obscure the desires of those situated on the margins. Staël demands, instead, that we employ a political process in our quest for general rules. With her model of engaged, loving, interdependent citizens, people must empathize, converse, argue—*yell* if necessary. This, for Staël, is the core of political debate. In order to enlist principles that really are best for an entire community, all must have knowledge and understanding of the needs, interests, and identities of various parts, factions, and sections of the community. Staël's insight that "general truths . . . are made up of *every fact* and *every individual being*" (OLB, 247, emphasis added) directs us toward the kind of polity that cannot ignore differences in private life in a quest for equality and liberty in political life.

Equality and liberty are meaningless if they are merely abstractions. Rousseau writes that the general will begins to deteriorate when "contradictory views and debates arise, and the best advice is not taken without question" (SC, IV:1, 275). Staël, in contrast, reminds us that the incommensurability of human goods is not a threat to politics, but rather an important part of its substance. She pointedly asks how equality and freedom can be meaningful *without* contradictory views and debates. Thus, Staël *redefines* reason in order to include passion, engagement, and interdependence (with certain identifiable others) as integral to moral political action.

Staël interprets the revolutionary call to transform and create moral citizens for the virtuous republic in a way that is able to recognize feminine desire. In *Considerations on the Principal Events of the French Revolution*, she emphasizes women's special political talent of persuading men to act within a more compassionate model of reason, according to rules of engagement, generosity, and compassion:

> It is the duty of *us women* at all times to aid individuals accused of political opinions of any kind whatsoever; for what are opinions in times of faction? Can we be certain that such and such events, such and such a situation, would not have changed our own views? and, if we except a few invariable sentiments, who knows how difference of situation might have acted on us? (CFR, II:III:XXV, 193, emphasis added).

Staël asks us to appeal to our emotions and to the sensuous imagination as a way to understand the situations of others in order to deliberate questions of justice that affect us all. She asks: "Can we be certain that such and such events, such and such a situation, would not have changed our own views?" Her question implies a deep suspicion of rigid principles, an intimate connection between losing the ability to love well, eschewing the employment of compassion in political debate, and a tyrannical politics that seeks to rise above the particulars of human lives. Staël wonders, then, whether our feelings might be more deeply rational than our intellect.

In her portrayal of Delphine, her female heroine who lives through the early stages of the Revolution, Staël brings to life her ideal of the good citizen. Delphine's confrontation with the judge who holds the fate of Lèonce in his hands succinctly captures the values of a loving citizen gendered as female. In an impassioned plea to the man who represents and interprets the laws of France, Delphine appeals simultaneously to the judge's sense of the universal humanity of the fighters on both sides of the political battle *and* to his ability to understand the facts of particular, individual lives and destinies, both his own and Lèonce's. Here the boundaries between reason and feeling are transgressed in a political, public venue. *Delphine* reminds us of the passionate grounding of rational discourse and the dangers of erasing or ignoring its presence.

Staël's reconstruction of what constitutes moral deliberation refigures the original call of the French Revolution for citizens to transform themselves in order to create a new political life. Staël brilliantly weaves together the personal and the political, the epistemology of love and reason, in pointing to men's (aristocratic, republican, and Napoleonic) failure to be good citizens and to the urgency to include women as citizens. Staël genders democratic morality as *female* in pointing to the explicit and urgent integration of the Revolution and its women. Staël's heroine, Delphine, both in spite of and because of her sex, wants to *participate* in defining the Revolution. She is a woman who fights to speak her mind in both love and politics while restructuring the realms of love and politics according to her moral standpoint.

5

Theorizing
Women's Desire

Staël's Corinne

·

In a strikingly painful passage of Germaine de Staël's famous novel *Corinne, or Italy*, Corinne asks her lover: "If society did not bind women with all manner of chains while men go unshackled, what would there be in my life to keep anyone from loving me?" (CI, XIV:IV, 271). Corinne is tormented by her lover's rejection and the reasons underlying it. The themes of Staël's novel, which link Corinne's lover's inability to love with Corinne's defiance of the social conventions that force women into particularly familial and private roles, reflect her preoccupation with the political effects of newly created gender roles in postrevolutionary France. *Corinne* was published in 1807; the time frame for the narrative is between 1794 and 1803. Set, as it is, during the Terror, and appearing in print during Napoleon's reign, Staël's novel was a timely affront to the politics that drove the draconian goals and methods of both Napoleon and the Jacobin revolutionaries.

In my interpretation, Corinne is a heroine who stretches the subversive gestures of the heroines we have already come to know—Sophie, Julie, Claire, and Delphine—further than any one of them were able to go. Corinne is not just *accused* of being an actress—she *is* an actress. Corinne has built her career (yes, a career!) on stretching the limits of her powers of imagination and subjectivity, on seeming to be someone she is not, on making herself into whoever she wants to be. Corinne's world is centered in feminine desire, theatricality, and appeal to the intimate commerce between men and women. In short, Staël fashions her most famous heroine to be all that Rousseau had warned against—all that makes women most dangerous, most subversive. She develops the practices of women to articulate a critique of the masculine public sphere and to make a gesture toward an alternative future.

Corinne's Story

In brief, the narrative of *Corinne, or Italy* is as follows: Corinne, a celebrated Italian artist and public persona with a mysterious past, meets Oswald Lord Nelvil, a conservative English gentleman, and they fall in love. Staël describes Corinne as "the most celebrated woman in Italy ... poet, writer, *improvisatrice*,[1] and one of the most beautiful women in Rome" (CI, II:I, 19). Extraordinarily talented and constantly in the public eye, Corinne is known to have the "most beautiful voice in Italy," to play tragedy like no other, to "dance like a nymph," and to compose original and charming drawings (CI, II:I, 20). Twenty-six years old and known only by her first name, Corinne has a mysterious past.[2] In taking only the name *Corinne*, she rejects her patriarchal lineage and recreates herself in her own imagination.

Oswald Lord Nelvil, Corinne's future lover, is described as "noble and handsome, [with] an important name [and] independent means" (CI, I:I,3). We meet Oswald at the beginning of the novel as he is traveling by boat from Edinburgh to Italy. Though Staël describes Oswald as "sensitive and passionate," she adds that "unhappiness and remorse" drives his "cheerless devotion to every duty" (CI, I:I,4). Wracked by grief and guilt over his father's death, Oswald is drawn to Corinne's open and receptive heart but has great difficulty accepting her independent ways and her presence as a public figure. As their relationship deepens, Oswald's increasing disapproval of Corinne's public role begins to stifle her talent.

The turning point of the novel occurs when Corinne finds it necessary to reveal the secret of her past to Oswald. Born and raised in England, she was once presented to Oswald's father as a possible mate for his son, but Oswald's father flatly refused. As an exceptional woman, Corinne was branded by the Englishman as an unacceptable wife. When Oswald learns of his late father's disapproval of the woman he loves, he becomes distraught and returns to England. While in his homeland, he meets and marries Corinne's half-sister Lucile, the woman Oswald's father originally intended him to marry. Lucille is a model of conventional femininity. The novel ends with Oswald's return to Italy with his new family in tow. Though Corinne is near death from grief because of Oswald's rejection, she and Lucile are reunited. On her deathbed Corinne bequeaths a complex legacy to women. She dies of unrequited love, but first she defies Oswald: she passes her talents on to her niece Juliette, Oswald's and Lucile's daughter.

Politics in Microcosm: Corinne at the Capitol

Corinne's public role is underscored by the venue and circumstances under which Corinne and Oswald first meet. When Oswald first arrives in Italy, he follows a crowd of Italians to the steps of the capitol where they are to honor the goddess, Corinne. Placed as Book II of *Corinne, or Italy*, the spectacle of Corinne's crowning in Rome, witnessed by scores of adoring citizens, represents Staël's reconfiguration of women's role in politics in microcosm. Oswald reflects on the possibilities inherent in Corinne's performance that day:

> Corinne's words at the Capitol had inspired a completely different idea: what if he could recover memories of his native land and at the same time gain a new life through the imagination; what if he could be reborn to the future and yet not break with the past? (CI, II:IV,33)

The idea of constructing a future while retaining the best of the past crops up continually in Staël's works.[3] Though Staël acknowledged that historically all political arrangements had been hostile to women ("In monarchies, women have ridicule to fear; in republics, hatred." [OLF, 201]), she felt that the best situation for women, post-Revolution, would be to maintain the influence women exercised under the monarchy while building the political institutions of the Republic. In her *Considerations on the Principal Events of the French Revolution*, Staël wrote:

> In England women are accustomed to be silent before men, when politics form the matter of conversation: in France women are accustomed to lead almost all the conversation that takes place at their houses, and their minds are early formed to the facility which that requires. Discussions on public affairs were thus softened by their means, and often intermingled with kind and lively pleasantry. (CFR, I:I:XVII, 380)

Indeed, as an Englishman, the adoration of a *woman* as an inspirational public figure was something entirely new to Oswald: "[N]othing could have been more opposed to an Englishman's customs and opinions than focusing the public eye on a woman's fortunes" (CI, I:I,19). Before seeing Corinne, Oswald learns from the crowd awaiting her that she is renowned for her "mind alone . . . heralding the union of all those gifts that captivate the imagination" (CI,I:I,20).

The qualities Staël instills in her character's mind pose an interesting and unique challenge to the politics of the day. In her discussion of Olympe de Gouges, Joan Scott underlines the significance of Staël's designation that Corinne was known especially for the power of her imagination. Scott notes:

> For a woman to claim the powers of creative imagination at the end of the eighteenth century was to posit something that was at once plausible and inconceivable in the terms of existing debates. For imagination was an increasingly troubling concept as philosophers grappled with, but did not resolve, its ambiguities.[4]

As Scott makes clear, men were calling upon their imagination, upon their "dreams" to invent new ways of life, new kinds of politics. But at that same time, questions were raised as to how these new ideas, which originated purely in the realm of the imaginary, were related to reason and reality. Moreover, ambiguity around the question of the relationship between imagination and reason (or reality) raised a host of other questions concerning the accuracy of representation more generally. Exactly what was the relationship between sign and its referent—politically, between the abstract citizen body and the concrete citizens to whom it referred? As Scott describes:

> The revolutionaries debated these questions endlessly. For some, the National Assembly was the nation; for others, it merely represented the nation. For some, elected representatives were delegates of the people; for others, they *were* the sovereign people. For some, the law was the general will; for others, it was an expression or reflection of that will; and so on. Epistemological problems *were* political problems. And the effort to settle them foundered on their ultimate unresolvability; whether representation accurately reflected a prior reality or created the very possibility of imagining such a reality could finally not be known, but the stakes in knowing were nonetheless high.[5]

Like Olympe de Gouge (in Scott's interpretation), Staël toys with the ambiguity of representation and the power of the imaginary to create Corinne as an admired woman, a *political* woman, best known for the powers of her imagination, especially her ability to create new ways of being in thought. Scott reminds us of the dangers that the philosophers associated with an active imagination, especially if it belonged to a woman:

> At its best, the active imagination could be directed to useful and enlightening ends. But there was always the danger of excess, for although the imaginative faculty might be susceptible to reason's regulation, it was not inherently reasonable. . . . The correction to the potential dangers of active imagination lay in the ever-vigilant, regulatory powers of reason. The line between fiction and reality, error and truth, madness and sanity, disorder and order needed constant policing by internal mechanisms of self-government. . . . The voice of reason is the voice of the (male) magistrate, the voice of the Law whose prohibitions regulate waking imagination. Order—both political and personal, the metaphor suggests—depends on the internalization of this law. The anarchy of dreams is figured as an attack by passion and desire on "the authority of the legislator" (a male figure, to be sure). The difference between day and night is the difference between order and chaos, reason and passion, discipline and desire, active and passive.[6]

Precisely because the imagination is so dangerous, so given to excess, and because it is associated with the feminine side of the self, it must constantly be regulated, constantly checked. Scott argues, for example, that though Rousseau indulged in the powers and seductions of the imaginary, the excesses of desire, he ultimately sought to "manage, if not eliminate the dangers of erotic excess" by restraining women's desire. In Scott's interpretation of Rousseau, the point of Sophie's training is to eliminate her desire such that she will serve only as "the screen upon which Emile can project his imagination."[7] As I have presented Sophie, however, she is far more able to recognize and act on her own desire as a woman (freed from the male imaginary) than has hitherto been acknowledged. Seeing this potential in Rousseau's women and Rousseau's sympathy with these feminine characters (as well as with the feminine within himself), I claim that when we look to Staël's characters, we find a development of the recognition of women's desires along these same lines.

In Staël's novel *Corinne,* we have a woman created in fiction who claims the power of citizenship in real life (blurring, again, those lines between fiction and reality). In rejecting her name and her homeland (England), Corinne refuses to internalize the law of the fathers. She goes even further in choosing and succeeding in a profession grounded in passion, desire, improvisation, imagination. As I have noted, Scott's comments indicate that Staël confronts the sexual politics of her own day in granting these powers to a woman.

Even more interesting, Corinne's talents prefigure contemporary feminist debates in psychoanalytic and political theory concerning the potential and power of the feminine imaginary. Luce Irigaray writes that the way the feminine is usually imagined within Western political thought and psychoanalysis is as Woman, a mere reflection of the man as his inferior or his opposite. According to Irigaray, men got Woman all wrong by using the wrong device in which to attempt to see her. Rather than see *her,* rather than recognize feminine desire, men saw *themselves,* but with an "essential" part missing. In criticizing Lacan, Irigaray asks why he used a flat mirror to view woman: the flat mirror "reflects the greater part of women's sexual organs only as a hole."[8] Clearly, a different sort of mirror is needed—specular or concave—so that the feminine is not represented merely as *lacking* the male penis.

With *Corinne,* Staël prefigures these debates in that Corinne consistently and confrontationally seeks to be seen outside the flat mirror. She wants to be seen and recognized in her own terms, as a *woman,* not as Woman limited by the male imagination. She has created herself anew. Upon her approach, Oswald observes: "She [Corinne] seemed at once a priestess of Apollo making her way toward the Temple of the Sun, and a woman perfectly simple in the ordinary relationships of life" (CI, I:I,21). Corinne exemplifies something entirely new, entirely different—both ordinary in private life and spectacular in public. As an *improvisatrice* (CI, II:I,19), even Corinne's language is original. Speaking of her at the capitol, Prince Castel-Forte, a friend of Corinne's, "called attention to the originality of Corinne's language, language so entirely born of her character and her way of feeling that no trace of affectation could ever alter a charm not only natural but involuntary as well" (CI, II:II, 24).[9] In all her talents, Corinne is "free of any compulsion to follow this style or that rule, Corinne [is] always herself, giving varied expression to the same power of imagination, the same magic of the arts in their various forms" (CI,II:I,25). In Corinne, "sound judgment and rapturous emotion, strength and gentleness combine in a single person" (CI,II:II,24). Moreover, Corinne's genius was acquired and inspired in peace at no one's expense or detriment:

> Corinne electrified Oswald's imagination. In his own country he had often seen statesmen borne in triumph by the people, but here, for the first time, he was witness to such homage paid a woman, a woman renowned only for the gifts of genius. Her triumphal chariot had cost not a single tear to anyone; and neither remorse nor fear checked admiration for those most beautiful gifts of nature: imagination, feeling, and thought. (CI, II:I,22)

Most interesting in this scene is Corinne's approval by all—men and women. She is presented as a political redemptress for Italy. Prince Castel-Forte deems Corinne "an offspring of the past, prophet of the future" (CI, II:II,25). In presenting Corinne as a public woman who transgresses the boundaries erected in both France and England—boundaries between men and women, language and poetry, reason and passion, judgment and emotion—Staël offers a glimpse of what she sees as possible in a truly democratic and culturally enlightened new France. Though the future is inspired by a woman in Staël's novel, she is quick to add that

> all the noted men of state approved: Yes, we would follow in her path; we would be as men as she is a woman, if like women, men could create a world in their own hearts, and if our genius—obliged to depend on social relationships and circumstances outside of the self—could catch fire at the touch of poetry alone. (CI, II:II, 25)

The Power of Poetry

It was no accident that Staël created her heroine as a great poet. Portraying Corinne as a public woman artist, a poet who knows the secrets of love, Staël extends a tradition within political philosophy linking the feminine, the artistic, and the erotic. Consider, for example, Socrates' argument against the poets in Book X of *The Republic*.[10] In conference with his friends of Athens, Socrates confirms that the best part of the soul, the part to be used for rational deliberation, is that which concerns itself with "measuring, counting, and weighing" (X:273). In contrast, poets appeal to the irrational elements in the soul. They inspire us to trust our experience, give in to our emotions, affirm the erotic, and yield to "womanish" behavior (X:277). Thus, if unable to defend themselves and poetry as beneficial to the polity (a defense Socrates finds highly unlikely), the poets should be banned from the city. Once the poets are banned, citizens will have need to

> behave like people who have fallen in love with someone but who force themselves to stay away from him, because they realize that their passion isn't beneficial. . . . Whenever we [hear poetry spoken] we'll repeat the argument we have just now put forward like an incantation so as to preserve ourselves from slipping back into that childish passion for poetry which the majority of people have. (X:279)

Plato understands that in appealing to our hearts, to eros, to the emotional parts of ourselves, poetry is very persuasive. This is precisely why he finds it so dangerous. Like the feminine, poetry represents chaos, passion, unruliness, disorder. The poet would have us identify with a cast of diverse characters, encourage us to feel their pain, encounter our own vulnerability in fearing that tragic events could happen to us too. Engaging with poetry sharpens our ability to empathize. Poetry forces us to recognize that we come from different backgrounds, have a variety of diverse experiences, and accord value to vulnerable and fleeting moments, persons, and experiences. Plato fears that acknowledgment of such diversity will disrupt the basis for a common language and the order characteristic of his ideal state. In response, he deems it necessary to ban from the public sphere both poets and women who don't act like men. In reducing all politics to rational calculation and claiming that all deliberation is best achieved by the unaided intellect, Plato comes close to eliminating even the possibility of experiencing passion.

Rousseau carries this tradition forward into modern philosophy. As we have seen in past chapters, Rousseau also links femininity, theatricality, inauthenticity, and sexual desire. In laying out the blueprint for his own republic, but with increased participation from qualified male citizens—a fraternity of men—Rousseau likewise finds it advantageous to ban the poets, the artists, and the playwrights from his polity. Rousseau is even more explicit than Plato about the necessary connection between women and the arts. Love is the primary subject matter in the theatre; love is the realm of women. If we allow the arts to flourish, we will necessarily "extend the empire of the fair sex, to make women and girls the preceptors of the public, and to give them the same power over the audience that they have over their lovers" (LD'A, 47). Worse yet, gender boundaries will blur. Rousseau worries that if women are allowed to participate in politics, men will become less manly:

> Every woman at Paris gathers in her apartment a harem of men more womanish than she . . . observe these same men, always constrained in these voluntary prisons, get up, sit down, pace continually back and forth to the fireplace, to the window, pick up and set down a fan a hundred times, leaf through books, glance at pictures, turn and pirouette about the room, while the idol, stretched out motionlessly on their couch, has only her eyes and her tongue active. (LD'A, 101)

This, of course, is the Rousseau we recognize from the *Letter to D'Alembert*. I have stressed, however, that there is an alternative Rousseau, a Rousseau we come to know by paying close attention to the women characters he creates and strongly identifies with. This is the Rousseau that Staël emulates when she creates Delphine and Corinne.

In creating a woman heroine, a poet who blurs the boundaries between man and woman, citizen and foreigner, reason and passion, Staël challenges the contours of the Revolution and its direction. Staël's portrait of Corinne, the public woman poet, was her own alternative vision, a vision of what politics could be, would be, if only we could value the feminine reinfused into the public sphere as a woman citizen.

We might ask, at this point, whether Staël's depiction of the feminine takes too great a risk. As I have argued, in ancient Greece and in revolutionary France (indeed, as today), the feminine is associated with the imaginary, the body, with excess, poetry, particularity (to name only the most obvious). It is almost as if, in embracing the stereotypes of the feminine in her characters, Staël assumes the ghettoization of women. As I pointed out earlier, in her defense of Marie-Antoinette, Staël appeals to the "hearts of women"; in *Delphine,* she portrays her character as emotional, as loving, as unwilling to sacrifice her ties and concerns for particular others for political goals. But has not this always been characterized as women's *problem,* precisely the reason for which women are excluded from the process of deliberating those abstract political goals? These "feminine" characteristics are ones that, men have argued, need to be suppressed within men (witness Rousseau's education of Emile, his depiction of Saint-Preux and Wolmar) to create the "manly" citizen. After all, Rousseau told us that men and women are different and codependent:

> Women's reason is practical and makes them very skillful at finding means for getting to a known end, but not at finding that end itself. . . . If woman could ascend to general principles as well as man can, and if man had as good a mind for details as woman does, they would always be independent of one another, they would live in eternal discord, and their partnership could not exist. (E, V:377)

Even in light of the discussion of Rousseau's women in preceding chapters, it is still disconcerting to admit an attraction to the feminine, if indeed it could possibly be construed as a mere reflection of the male self, as a writing of the feminine by the masculine. How could a recognition of some truth in this statement possibly be a strategy for subversion of the gender roles that create manly citizenship and keep women from having any voice in political life? Does Staël's willingness, even eagerness, to claim these characteristics for women merely reinscribe traditional and mythical gender roles? Irigaray would argue that Staël is not reverting to old stereotypes, but rather moving forward, ahead of her time:

> One must assume the feminine role deliberately. Which means already to convert a form of subordination into an affirmation, and thus begin to thwart it. . . . To play with mimesis is thus, for a woman, to try to recover the place of her exploitation by discourse, without allowing herself to be simply reduced to it. It means to resubmit herself—inasmuch as she is on the side of the "perceptible," of "matter"—to "ideas," in particular to ideas about herself, that are elaborated in/by a masculine

logic, but so as to make "visible," by an effect of playful repetition, what was supposed to remain invisible: the cover-up of a possible operation of the feminine in language. It also means "to unveil" the fact that, if women are such good mimics, it is because they are not simply resorbed in this function. *They also remain elsewhere.*[11]

According to Irigaray, the problem for women is that the feminine is always signified as excess, as outside the symbolic order, but yet women are not in fact outside the society we live in, but rather very much a part of it. Rousseau makes this quite visible in *La Nouvelle Héloïse*: Julie is the dangerous insider. And like but beyond Rousseau, Staël adopts a strategy of representing the feminine that confronts and questions the value of the symbolic and of the society in which we live. Better than Rousseau, she offers a more developed alternative.

Women Invade the Public Sphere

Geneviève Fraisse writes that "a woman's entry into public life and the recognition of her freedom in matters of love were signs of danger because they comprised the two arenas where a woman could achieve autonomy as an individual."[12] Staël's heroine, Corinne, threatens to achieve this autonomy in both areas. Two moments early in Corinne and Oswald's relationship illustrate. After having spent uninterrupted, intense time together with Oswald, Corinne starts to feel some discomfort from the lack of public/social engagement. She accepts an invitation to a ball. Oswald is "annoyed" (CI, VI:I, 90) that she has agreed to attend and becomes even more annoyed when he recognizes the happiness and fulfillment Corinne gains from public recognition:

> How charming and dignified Corinne was at that moment! How much a sovereign as she knelt! And when she rose, sounding her instrument, her airy cymbal, she seemed quickened by an enthusiasm for life, for youth, and for beauty which must have made it seem that to be happy she needed no one else. Alas! that was not the situation; but Oswald was afraid, and though he admired her, he sighed as if each one of her successes had separated her from him! . . . Trying to hide his distress, his fascination, and his suffering, he [Oswald] managed to say: "Well Corinne, what homage, what success! But among all those men who worship you so enthusiastically, is there one brave and reliable friend? Is

there a lifelong protector? And should the vain uproar of applause be enough for a soul like yours?" (CI, VI:I, 93)

The second example is a moment when Corinne and Oswald attend a music recital wherein Corinne is immediately recognized. Recalling her appearance at the capitol, the crowd begins to shout: "Vive, Corinne!" Corinne is visibly moved by the public display of affection, but Oswald interprets her happiness as usurping private emotions that he feels should exist and be displayed only for him. He reprimands Corinne:

"Madam, you must not tear yourself away from such success; it is as good as love, since it makes your heart beat so hard." Without waiting for her reply, he went off to take a seat at the far end of the box. Corinne was sorely troubled by his words that in one moment robbed her of all the pleasure she had taken in triumphs she was happy to have him witness. (CI, IX:II, 164)

Unable to tolerate Corinne's public life any longer, Oswald justifies his rejection of Corinne by separating the private woman from the public figure. Steeped in the ways of the society he was raised in, Oswald cannot help but see Corinne as either a woman needing the protection of a man or a public figure immune to the emotions of a woman.[13] Though Corinne has clearly warned Oswald of the "unfathomed depths of sorrow" (CI, IV:VI, 75) that lie in her soul, Oswald rejects her by ignoring her feelings as a sensitive woman. Surely, Oswald muses, a celebrated public figure like Corinne does not have the feelings of a woman.

It is Corinne's difference from other women that both attracts Oswald and keeps him from loving her fully. Corinne's talent and public role remind Oswald all too often of his father's rejection of Corinne as a wife for him. It is Lucile, Corinne's English half-sister, that Oswald's father had found acceptable. Faced with Oswald's attraction to Lucile, Corinne finds herself wondering about her own merit and identity. In looking at Lucile through Oswald's eyes, Corinne feels embarrassed by the uses to which she has put her talents and her developed mind. In fact, she wonders how Oswald could possibly resist Lucile's charms— she is beautiful, pleasant, unassuming, seemingly content with Woman's role in a male-dominated society.

Lucile exemplifies the model of woman highly esteemed in the ideology that any public role for women was seen as a perversion of nature. As Margaret Darrow notes, in the early nineteenth century many noblewomen who themselves had played an active public role voluntarily adopted this new model of womanhood. Because the excesses of the ancien régime were seen as intricately tied to the moral waywardness of women who did not see their family ties as conjugal and affective, public women were called on to redirect their talents toward the role of "directress and manager of domestic affairs."[14] Staël points out that ultimately this is why Lucile, not Corinne, gets the man. In charting Corinne's demise upon losing the love of Oswald, Staël condemns Oswald's male gaze that forces Corinne to feel humiliated by her deviance from Lucile's example of womanhood. And just as masculine ideology destroyed the early goals of the Revolution, so the maleness of Oswald's gaze eventually destroys them all.

Exceptional Woman, Unacceptable Wife

Staël clearly demonstrates that if Oswald had married Corinne, the outcome would have been just as bad.[15] If Oswald had deemed Corinne Woman enough to love as a wife, she would have lost her identity as a public figure, poet, and artist. Oswald's masculine gaze destroys Corinne regardless of whether he rejects her or tries to incorporate her into his world. Since Oswald is only able to love Corinne when idealizing her in his mind as the proper natural Woman, his qualified love usurps her talent and obliterates her identity. Oswald's commitment to honoring his father's view of the world while forging a new world for himself would have destroyed the fabric of who Corinne is and must be. Corinne recognizes the problem early in her courtship with Oswald. Having "cut herself off completely from society to devote all her time to her feelings for Oswald" (CI, VI:I, 89), Corinne begins to feel that she is suffocating:

> [Corinne]: "To feel dominated by a single affection as I do can be rewarding only in private life. Loving you as I do does me great harm: I need my talents, my mind, my imagination to sustain the brilliance of the life I have adopted." [Oswald]: "You mean that for me you would not give up the homage, the glory . . ." (CI, VI:I, 90)

Despite his best efforts to love Corinne, Oswald does not know how to love in a way that would allow Corinne to grow personally and publicly, or artistically, in their love. For Oswald, women are not meant to be public persons; women must sacrifice all other interests for private love and emotion. Thus, the kind of love Oswald offers Corinne is a love that has no room for her identity as a public woman. Without appearing dogmatic, Oswald believes, à la the dominant interpretation of Rousseau, that a public woman is an aberration, someone to be condemned. In loving a woman like Corinne, a man like Oswald must destroy her public persona. According to the narrator, "Corinne was wrong to cast her lot with a man who could only thwart her natural self, and repress rather than stimulate her gifts" (CI, XVI:I, 303). This is precisely what happens as Oswald and Corinne's love intensifies and Oswald is forced to ask Corinne to make sacrifices that are impossible if she is to retain her artistic voice.

Thus Corinne's choice: she could be Oswald's lover or be a public artist. Both, however, are a part of herself; both express her desires. Oswald and Corinne lose by having this choice imposed on Corinne. Staël's critique of the revolutionary fashioning of gender boundaries confirms that when man/citizen and woman/wife are constructed as opposing, mirror image categories, both men and women lose. In portraying a woman as an esteemed artist in her novel and framing Corinne's dilemma as a split consciousness about her identity, Staël is eager to point out the travesty in denying women the ability to be women when (and *if*) they are able to become public figures. In Staël's novel, Corinne is only able to retain her public identity if she is able to deny her feelings and desires as a woman. She cannot be both woman and citizen simultaneously. Herein lies Staël's critique of having to choose between equality and difference. As Joan Scott writes:

> The intensity of feminist politics—of feminist actions and antifeminist reactions—follows from the undecidability of sexual difference. So does the paradoxical quality of feminist claims for rights. Drawn into arguments about sameness or difference that they did not initiate, [feminists] . . . took on the group identity attributed to them even as they refused its negative characteristics. . . . On the one hand, they [feminists]

seemed to accept authoritative definitions of gender; on the other hand, they refused those definitions.[16]

Caught in the midst of universal claims for equality but denying such claims for women, Germaine de Staël is clearly one such feminist. She found herself in the awkward position of recognizing and living women's difference (her own difference) while simultaneously desiring women's active participation in the moral and political debates of the day. She seeks to move beyond forcing a choice of equality versus difference by demonstrating, in Corinne, the travesty that occurs in the wake of forcing such choices.

Staël's work points out, in both *Delphine* and *Corinne,* that feminists need not fear a recognition of sexual difference. Though Rousseau's conclusions concerning women were that women's difference from men necessitates their seclusion in the private sphere while men seek a common equality in public, had he developed a concept of citizenship based on his female characters, he might have come to entirely different conclusions. In previous chapters I have shown that Rousseau's "solution"—political equality amongst men—does not even work for men: they destroy women in the process. In seeking to move beyond a male-centered concept of equality and sameness, Jane Flax argues:

> Domination arises out of an inability to recognize, appreciate and nurture differences, not out of a failure to see everyone as the same. Indeed, the need to see everyone the same in order to accord them dignity and respect is an expression of the problem, not a cure for it. Since the fundamental problem with gender is that, as currently constituted, it is a relation of domination, feminists should seek to end domination—not gender, not differences and certainly not the feminine.[17]

It is the denigration of the feminine that Staël finds most abhorrent. Recall that Staël was attracted to Rousseau primarily because Rousseau was able to portray and esteem the feminine with such eloquence. Yet in a crucial break with Rousseau, Staël suggests, through her novel, that these feminine values, clearly associated with diversity, freedom of expression, passion, and empathy, should be regarded as appropriate for the public sphere. Virginia Sapiro makes an important distinction between "'citizens who happen to be women' and representing women 'because they are women.'"[18] As such, women as women bring values to public life that Staël argues are of utmost importance to a vibrant public sphere, a public sphere that does not reduce incommensurable values to a single standard of calculation and measuring, a public sphere able to listen to, and accommodate, diverse voices and ways of life, expressed metaphorically in a respect for the arts.

This was not the kind of public sphere constructed in France in the wake of the Revolution. Describing revolutionary politics, Joan B. Landes reminds us that "the Republic was constructed against women, not just without them."[19] The bourgeois male values retained as crucial in the new Republic required the exclusion of women as women. In *The Sexual Contract*, Carole Pateman insists that in the founding of a bourgeois republic, the concept of fraternity applies strictly to males. Fraternity does not, in Pateman's estimation, imply a community that might theoretically include women: "Men must have their own social and political clubs so that they can educate themselves politically and reinforce their citizenship, out of the reach of women and their weakening, subversive influence" (99).

The metaphor of Corinne's impending loss of her public voice is alarming. Corinne believes herself to be powerless in the face of her destiny as a Woman. As she and Oswald fall more deeply in love, Corinne's talents fade. This process begins as Corinne feels pressure to reveal to Oswald her patriarchal ties. Oswald's great hope for Corinne is that love will bind her again to his great fatherland and that she will "prefer domestic happiness" over the "luster" of her genius (CI, XV:I, 275). Oswald's desire that Corinne choose domestic bliss over her public life and artistic talent serves to split Corinne's psyche in a very painful way. The result is Corinne's demise. First, she completely loses her ability to speak or perform in public, signifying the erosion of her public voice:

> For all her extraordinary gifts of language, she would hesitate over the choice of words, occasionally using an expression without the slightest connection to what she meant to say. Then she would laugh at herself, her eyes filling with tears through the laughter. (CI, XV:II, 277)

In hoping to win Oswald's favor, Corinne "dreaded whatever seemed to deviate from the domestic way of life so dear to Lord Nelvil"

(CI, XVI:I, 303). But she is who she is—an extraordinary woman, a woman who transgresses the boundaries of conventional femininity—and she cannot bear to abandon part of her identity. Nevertheless, when Corinne feels her love with Oswald is secure, her ability to perform intensifies. When hoping to please Oswald, she is at a loss for words, but when she knows that she pleases him because he loves her unconditionally, she performs at her best.[20] Her last performance in front of Oswald comes at a time and in a place (Venice) when they feel destined to be together. The Venetians ask her to perform in a comedy. Corinne appears in this play as an Amazon Queen, ruling over men. Her happiness is "dazzling"; her performance unparalleled: "[A]ll the spectators rose to applaud Corinne as the true queen" (CI, XVI:II, 306). At this moment of sovereignty in love, art, and politics, Corinne's destiny as a Woman cruelly reaches out to claim her. Oswald informs her that his regiment has been called up and that he is leaving immediately for England without her. Upon comprehending the ramifications of this news, Corinne falls unconscious, hits her head, and awakes bloody and disheartened:

> She noticed her pale drawn face in a mirror, and her bloodstained, disheveled hair. "Oswald, Oswald, I was not like this the day you met me at the Capitol. On my forehead I wore the crown of hope and glory, now it is stained with blood and dust." (CI, XVI:III, 308)

From this point forward, Staël's novel traces Corinne's impending destruction and death. Oswald returns to England, marries Lucile, and, after many years, returns to Italy with his wife Lucile and their daughter Juliette. This turns out to be too much for Corinne to bear. Rejected, destroyed, and driven by revenge, Corinne manages to reconcile with Lucile and teach Juliette her poetic talents. Despite the revenge she wreaks through managing to forever torment Oswald with the memory of "Corinne, the exceptional woman" living on in his daughter, Corinne ultimately dies.

What are we to make of this conclusion to the novel? A strong public woman dying of love for a man who rejects her hardly seems a feminist story. Yet in interweaving Corinne's private dilemma of identity (her split consciousness) with a condemnation of a public sphere and of the model of manly citizenship that will not accommodate the feminine (other than as Woman), Staël drives home the point that gender boundaries that restrict our identities inevitably affect the kind of politics we practice. Rousseau had thought he could construct a democracy, a fraternal order, that would maintain a respect for femininity at home and masculinity in public. But both Rousseau's private and public spheres turn out to be sorely lacking. Compelled as they are to suppress all feminine aspects of their personality in seeking to reduce all values to the standard of the "common man," Rousseau's men do not make good citizens. And likewise, Rousseau's women, like Corinne, ironically end up having to be killed for their desire to expand their own identities beyond the narrow confines of "wife" and "mother."

As a woman artist, a public persona, Staël's heroine Corinne embodies all that a democracy might be. For Staël, a true democracy tolerates, even encourages, diverse points of view, the conflict of values, and the challenge that poetry entails to a set moral order. In portraying an exceptional woman as the force for bringing these qualities to light, Staël maintains the connection between femininity, the arts, poetry, and the erotic. In bringing these values directly into the public sphere, Staël reminds us that we should respect these aspects of ourselves if we are to actually practice democratic politics. Attempting to get Corinne to conform to masculine values, to the way the masculine constructs the feminine, results in her death.

Staël Refashions the Values of Public Life

Staël was an active participant in the political struggles of the day through her political essays and novels and through the intellectual and political discourse in her salon in Paris and, after her exile, in Coppet.[21] Yet she had to struggle constantly to create space for herself and other women. As a woman who sought to transform the model of femininity to include the participation of women in politics and the public sphere, Staël was faced with having to deny her femininity in order to participate like men (in public) or to deny her identity as a writer and public figure in order to fulfill her desires as a woman.

Staël seeks to move beyond this conundrum that constrains women's identity, and in doing so, she brilliantly recreates the values of public

6

Conclusion

Recognizing Women

•

The world around me was harmoniously based on fixed coordinates and divided into clear-cut compartments. No neutral tints were allowed: everything was in black and white; there was no intermediate position between the traitor and the hero, the renegade and the martyr: all inedible fruits were poisonous; I was told that I "loved" every member of my family, including my most ill-favoured great-aunts. All my experience belied this essentialism. White was only rarely totally white, and the blackness of evil was relieved by lighter touches; I saw greys and half-tones everywhere. Only as soon as I tried to define their muted shades, I had to use words, and I found myself in a world of bony-structured concepts. Whatever I beheld with my own eyes and every real experience had to be fitted somehow or other into a rigid category: the myths and the stereotyped ideas prevailed over the truth: unable to pin it down I allowed truth to dwindle into insignificance.

——SIMONE DE BEAUVOIR, *Memoirs of a Dutiful Daughter*

Novels give a false idea of mankind, it has been said. This is true of bad novels, as it is true of paintings which imitate nature badly. When novels are good, however, nothing gives such an intimate knowledge of the human heart as these portrayals of the various circumstances of private life and the impressions they inspire. Nothing gives so much play to reflection, which finds much more to discover in details than in generalities. . . . The most truthful account is always an imitative truth.

——GERMAINE DE STAËL, *Essay on Fictions*

In the passage quoted above, Simone de Beauvoir remembers a painful moment of discovery. As a young child, de Beauvoir writes, she felt that the world she knew, the experiences she felt powerfully and truthfully, could not be expressed by the words she had been taught. Her truth was not one of black and white, but one of "greys and half-tones," "muted shades" reflecting a messy, misshapen existence, a reality that did not fit easily into "clear-cut compartments" described by "bony-structured concepts." Staël elaborates on this idea in noting that novels are better than other mediums at getting at the truth of life's unpredictable ebbs and flows. Novels, Staël writes, provide an "intimate knowledge of the human heart." The "circumstances of private life and the impressions they inspire" give play to a kind of "reflection" that grounds truth in particular details and intimate experience, in Staël's eyes, a truth more honest than "generalities."

Remembering her early attraction to the articulation of a conflict between a "love of general political ideals" and "attachment to particular human beings," Martha Nussbaum says that though she was always interested in "pursuing questions called philosophical," it seemed best to her "to discuss the issues in connection with a text that displayed concrete lives and told a story; and to discuss them in ways that responded to these literary features."[1]

In Rousseau's and Staël's novels we have listened to stories of exclusion from communities constituted by the simultaneous denial of, and need for, the bodies of actual women. The stories of these women's lives warn against adopting the model of "manly" citizen that emerged from basic tenets of Enlightenment thought. In weaving the personal with the political, the literary with the philosophical, and the particular with the universal, these women's stories shore up the dangers of ignoring the voices of those designated too passionate, too loyal to concrete others, unable to pursue abstract philosophical goals. Page du Bois has written that "women interrupt the scene of philosophy with hysterical crying, with mourning, beating their breasts, inappropriate behaviors of all sorts."[2]

Women are unwilling to leave the "private"—the body, the family, sexuality, and desire—behind when reflecting on the truths of their lives in political and philosophical context. These private reflections have most often been confined to the pages of literature because of the disruptive effects they are believed to have on general philosophical truths. Like Simone de Beauvoir's reminder that "experience belies essentialism," and that "rigid categories" give way to "myths" and "stereotyped ideas," Rousseau's and Staël's women find that their experience, too, fits uneasily into the confines of the general will and the ideological excesses of the French Revolution. The stories of these women urge us to reevaluate the politics of a philosophical tradition that demands that we ignore particular lives, to reject the kind of equality that designates difference in pejorative terms, and to construct a democratic space and a democratic politics that is able to deal with conflicting loyalties, incommensurable goods, and cross-cutting identities.

Gestures Toward (Un)manly Citizenship

If we keep on speaking the same language together, we're going to reproduce the same history. Begin the same old stories all over again. Don't you think so? Listen: all round us, men and women sound just the same. The same discussion, the same arguments, the same scenes. The same attractions and separations. The same difficulties, the same impossibility of making connections. The same . . . . Same . . . Always the same.   —LUCE IRIGARAY, "When Our Lips Speak Together"

No one answers me, but it may be that someone hears.
    —GERMAINE DE STAËL, *Delphine*

By way of a concluding reminder of the ways in which Rousseau's and Staël's women sketch an alternative democratic politics, I want to bring the discussion back to the central metaphors of this book: Sophie at the dinner party, Julie on her deathbed, Delphine in the judge's chamber, and Corinne at the capitol. We have seen that each woman, solely by virtue of being a woman, is in danger of being ignored, dismissed, sent away, or forgotten. At the same time, we have seen that these women have things on their minds that they would like to say. Their words have not been said before; indeed, if and when they were said, they were quickly appropriated by those who sought to make them appear insignificant, beside the point, bizarre, even insane.

Throughout the previous chapters, I have sought out and directed our attention toward such gestures. I argued that it is no surprise that these gestures are made by women, for women are usually constructed within philosophical texts as the excessive feminine "other," the ground for the possibility of male citizenship and its ever-present threat for disruption. Rousseau and Staël depict women who confronted the age designated as the Age of Reason—an age obsessed with defining categories, delineating identities, marking progress, measuring virtue. Iris Marion Young has written that if one is interested in an emancipatory politics, one must decisively reject modern traditions of moral and political thought formulated during the age of reason. She explains that the definition of reason was integrally connected to the designation of who could and who could not be involved in the political process:

> Modern political theorists and politicians proclaimed the impartiality and generality of the public and at the same time quite consciously found it fitting that some persons, namely women, nonwhites and sometimes those without property, be excluded from participation in that public. . . . By assuming that reason stands opposed to desire, affectivity and the body, the civic public must exclude bodily and affective aspects of human existence. In practice this assumption forces a homogeneity of citizens upon the civic public. It excludes from the public those individuals and groups that do not fit the model of the rational citizen who can transcend body and sentiment.[3]

Young is right about the Enlightenment's concerted attempt to construct the rational citizen and the designation of who was to be excluded for reasons of not conforming to this model. Indeed, the model was that of the "manly" citizen. It may be, however, that the triumph of this model of manly citizenship (by liberals, communitarians, and feminists, each from a different critical perspective) has been proclaimed too quickly. When I say this, I do not mean to imply that women and others were not excluded from the rights of citizenship. The deep roots of misogyny and xenophobia in philosophy were in most cases enacted and embodied in political spheres. In this case the heroes of the French Revolution, from the Jacobins to Napoleon, were able to successfully control, if not silence, critical voices. Women who strove to gain the rights of equality promised by the universalist rhetoric of the French Revolution were forced to choose between equality on male terms and difference as defined by deviance from the male measure. Hence, we understand Staël's philosophical commitment to individuality and singular eccentricity as combined with her willingness to make claims for women as a political category brought into being by women's very exclusion from the political process. Staël emphatically thought it possible, indeed pressing, to make claims on behalf of women divorced from an accompanying commitment to women as an essential category of identity defined by men.

I have claimed that this possibility arises out of a respect for the kind of feminine difference attributed to the women described by Rousseau. The readings of Rousseau as misogynist versus the readings that claim his respect for difference as complementarity again mirror this false dualism between "men's" and "women's" terms. Though the goal of the age of reason was to secure identity, enforce strict gender boundaries, and conclusively construct the borders of citizenship in terms of a manly identity, critical voices remained, even within some of the texts where these goals were most vigorously pursued.

There is always *more* than the man in the text. Though Rousseau is indeed (in)famous for his faith in manly citizenship, the reading I have advanced demonstrates that neither masculinity nor citizenship are fixed in his work as coherent, intact, or stable categories. Women's desire, especially as formulated and enacted in political action (even when that "political" action is within the home, as is the case with Rousseau's women) threatens the identity of the manly citizen at every turn. Indeed, the feminine within each manly citizen turns out to be an ever-present and potentially subversive presence. As Linda Zerilli reminds us:

> The disorderly woman is indeed *dis*-ordering—albeit not in ways anticipated by the theorist: she disrupts the whole structure of binary oppositions (e.g., private/public, feminine/masculine, nature/culture) that political theorists articulate in their frantic efforts to contain the play of signification; she interrupts and animates the longing for closure and coherence, unity and commonality.[4]

The disorderly women I discovered are located in unlikely texts (authored during the triumphant moments of Enlightenment reason), and they speak within a surprising variety of contexts and structures. Their actions remind us of the amazing diversity of ways that women express dissatisfaction, frustration, and the desire that beckons beyond critique. None of these women are simple mirrors of male ego, nor do they represent a mere lack of manly attributes. They are women whose words and actions beg us to see beyond the "flat" mirror held by the male subject, to move beyond the model of the manly citizen. Juliet Flower Mac-Cannell argues that when we look to women as subjects of their own desire, we see a different picture than we are trained to perceive:

> The woman as other, as partner, as sharing the same fate and taking the same chances, as erotic. The woman as "perfect," a gleaming, smooth "object" of desire, a curtain between us and destiny: these are the [usual] choices. Can we continue to take women as *objects* of desire, machines for the pleasure of reproduction as well as sites of destruction? . . . the unmarked other—the other who could have been the *subject* of their own passion: the anonymous masses, the colonized, women, those without the "phallus"—is the crucial piece missing.[5]

The women we have encountered in this text are indeed the "crucial piece missing." Their lives reach toward a radical alterity; their method of knowing, speaking, and being is a foreign presence within philosophy. Though Rousseau claims that "to find [Sophie] it is necessary to know her," (E, V: 357), we discovered that it is instead Sophie who desires and finds Emile, that the Woman Rousseau "knows" is not really Sophie at all. Unlike Emile, who assumes that his single will can represent the will of all, Sophie teaches us the value of searching out diverse, contradictory, even angry, voices that make competing claims on the general will. Describing how the man and the woman act differently at the dinner party, Rousseau makes clear that it is the woman who is able to listen for discordant or unwilling contributions. Though Rousseau's Saint-Preux commends unmediated and perfect understanding ("How many things were said without opening the lips! How many ardent sentiments were transmitted without the cold agency of speech!" [J, V:III, 459]), Julie herself, on her deathbed, notes that "nothing hurts women as much as silence!" (J, VI:XI, 579). Julie is keenly aware of her unmet desires: she complains to Claire of Wolmar's lack of interest in their marriage and the children, as well as of the pain she feels because of Wolmar's insistence that she accept her former lover into their household as tutor to the children. Julie's most intense passions, unmet by Saint-Preux and Wolmar, are reserved for her cousin Claire. Rousseau describes a moment in *La Nouvelle Héloïse* when Julie and Claire are reunited:

> Opening the door of her room, I saw Julie seated facing the window and holding little Henriette on her knees, as she often did. Claire had prepared a big speech after her manner laced with sentiment and levity; but as she set foot on the threshold of the room, the speech, the levity, were all forgot; she flew to her friend shouting in an indescribable rapture: Cousin, forever, forever until death! . . . The joy, the commotion seized Julie to such a point, that having arisen and extending her arms with a very sharp cry, she sank back into the chair and swooned. . . . [Claire] rushed to assist the helpless Julie, and fell onto her in the same condition. (J, V:V, 491)

The intense emotion of these two women would not be so remarkable were it not set in the midst of the wooden, formal, completely impoverished relationship that Julie experiences with the men in her life. Even Saint-Preux runs roughshod over his love for Julie in his deliberate quest to be *seen* to fulfill public duty. Julie scoffs at Saint-Preux's ridiculous reverence for honor, but disappointment and pain lie just below the surface.

The hierarchy between public virtue and private desire so bluntly proclaimed by the men in Julie's life obscures Julie's desires and creates the conditions for a plethora of distinct examples of the way that "equality," structured on male terms, obscures women's "different" needs. Staël's Delphine, too, notes that the oppressive nature of what is claimed to be open dialogue is "hardly noticeable in the ordinary course of life, but when one must deal with inherently troubling subjects, one is astonished at the pain inflicted by the clear, direct language that in no way alters the situation, but torments the imagination almost as much as a new grief" (D, IV:23, 318).

Staël's women reinforce the inadequacy of conceptions of an autonomous and stable self, a unified community will, and disembodied deliberation. Central to Staël's critique of the French Revolution is the insight that justice is never served when we lose sight of individual lives. Delphine's plea to the judge advances the idea that we must fully consider our emotional ties and our human attachments to irreplaceable others in order to make just decisions. When the judge admits to the passionate zeal of the Revolutionary Tribunal, we are forced to compare the partisan perspective of a "general" will with the loyalties we are asked to ignore when making political decisions. Corinne's consciousness as a public woman unwilling to ignore one of her identities (as artist) for the sake of another (to be Oswald's wife) speaks to the irrationality of the attempt at a unified identity and points to the political loss incurred when the voices of women and the marginalized are ignored. Staël makes this point explicit in her defense of Marie-Antoinette, a woman she believes was vilified by public opinion solely because of her visibility as a public woman:

> Braving public opinion is an extremely dangerous course for women to take; it is necessary, in order to dare to do such a thing, that they make themselves feel—to use a poetic comparison—*a tripled band of brass around the heart*, to make it inaccessible to the blows of calumny, and to concentrate within itself all of the heat of its sentiments; it is necessary to have the strength to renounce the world, to possess the resources which will permit [women] to pass through the world. (D, II:7, 116)

Staël realized that it was hardly likely that the excluded would possess the resources, the strength, the resolve, and the will to brave public opinion by making their discontent known. Delphine notices that the voices of others must be sought out in order to be heard:

> Yes, in all of life's relationships, in all the countries of the world, one must live among the oppressed; half of all feelings and ideas are missing in the fortunate and the powerful. (D, IV:23, 318)

Staël insists that we not take silence as approval, that any conception of democracy must implore, indeed require, its citizens to locate and listen to the voices and concerns of those most unlikely to speak out. When we are able to recognize autonomous feminine desire (embodied in feminine subjectivity) as demonstrated in Rousseau's women, we are forced to think through the ways that political arrangements modeled on male equality fail to accommodate the desire (difference) of women. A model of equality that treats all the same simply cannot recognize the individuality of each. Listen again to Rousseau's Saint-Preux describe Julie's "maxims" concerning equality:

Man, she said, is too noble a being to have to serve merely as an instrument of others, and he ought not to be used for purposes that suit them without consulting also what suits him; for men are not made for positions, but positions are made for them, and in order to allocate things appropriately one must not in distributing them look for the job each man is best at, but for the one that is best for each man, so as to render him as good and happy as is possible. It is never permissible to degrade a human soul for the benefit of others, nor to make a villain for the service of honest people. (J, V:II, 439)

This insight demands that we look at the potential of each individual, that we allow and insure that each be accorded what Drucilla Cornell has called the "primary good of self-respect."[6] Persons are to be treated as singular individuals, as ends in themselves, worthy of happiness. This reverence for individuality can be expanded to develop a respect for feminine difference, a difference read outside male terms. When we lament, as we do, the deaths of Sophie and Julie at the hands of the virtuous society utterly unable to recognize their voices, we must stop and evaluate the ethical import of the collectivity that claims the moral force of a general will and the value of claims that conceive difference solely in pejorative terms.

A respect for difference that ethically rejects domination is given political content by the words and gestures that define this difference as well as the space this difference inhabits. A crucial component of this respect for difference is the unwillingness to reject embodiment as well as the loyalty we feel for particular others in our lives. Each woman in this text recognizes herself as an embodied being, constituted by her relationship to others, her place in history, her commitment to family members and to the concerns of those who are marginalized by the "whole." We have watched Sophie and Julie, Delphine and Corinne reject the impulse to place commitment to the general will and loyalty and love for particular others within a hierarchical grid. This refusal to embrace the communitarian dream of the transparent and unified whole, however, is not abandoned for (but rather *constituted by*) the competing mass of individual wills and power politics. The women in this text are baffled by this choice, and they replace the dualism with an ethical and loving commitment to individuals that can only be respected within a polity that pursues humanitarian (group) goals in light of the demands for (and commitment to) social justice. Sophie's commitment to her children, Julie's passion for Saint-Preux and Claire, Delphine's loyalty to Léonce, and Corinne's love for Oswald exemplify each woman's desire to love individuals and honor loyalties in the kind of political space that also (and simultaneously) honors the needs of the whole by seeking the voices and criticisms of the downtrodden. Rousseau's Saint-Preux applauds the way Julie loves and respects family, friends, neighbors, and strangers:

> She inquires about the needs of her neighborhood with the warmth she puts into her own interests; she knows all its inhabitants; she extends to it, so to speak, her family circle. (J, V:II, 436)

Likewise, Sophie is baffled by Emile's claim that he must choose between his love for her and the rights of humanity; Julie is stifled by the demands of Wolmar's (and the community's) virtue, which insists on the refusal of her passionate love for her friends; Delphine risks the censure of a moralizing community in order to assist women friends who defy models of conventional femininity; and Corinne rejects her past and her patriarchal lineage to create an artist's community of friends pursuing creative fulfillment. The choices these women make, within a context of extremely limited options, propel each toward the destruction of their creative impulse, culminating in their deaths. Because they live within polarized worlds (within tragic novels), these women are not allowed to live out their alternative visions modeled on their own sense of self.

I have argued, however, that their "failure" need not imply dismay and defeat. Our sympathy as readers for their lives and goals demands that we critically reconstruct a world in which these women could live as creative and fulfilled selves. Each woman makes it clear that the only way for the feminine self to have an independent and self-directed vision of the good is not to have to choose between various and conflicting models of identity (bad girl/good girl, artist/wife, whore/Woman). Moreover, as citizens, these women do not construe loyalty to family and loyalty to community as conflicting. Instead, love for family and intimate friends becomes a model for the care, respect, and justice desired by all.

→→ · ←←

Following Rousseau in his conviction that "depictions of love always make a greater impression than the maxims of wisdom" (LD'A, 54), we must be willing to affirm at least two conclusions after considering the gestures and words of the fictional women in these texts. First, in sympathizing with their fate, we are moved to reject the requirements for citizenship, indeed even the ways of knowing, that exclude these women and the "difference" by which they are marked. And second, in appealing to our hearts, we might be moved to consider alternatives for citizenship beyond the cold confines of objectivity, general will, and manly citizenship. To learn from the words and experiences of these fictional women, to honor feminine difference, we must write alternative ends to these stories.

NOTES

·

INTRODUCTION
Imagining Woman

1. Denise Riley, *"Am I That Name?" Feminism and the Category of 'Women' in History* (Minneapolis: University of Minnesota Press, 1988) points out that *Woman,* with a capital letter, has served to alert us to the dangers of essentializing women's experiences. She adds, however, that we must also beware of the problems in leaving the more modest-sounding *woman* and *women* unexamined. Within this text, I use Woman (capitalized and without quotation marks) to designate an idealization of feminine characteristics within the history of Western philosophy, women and woman (lower case and without quotation marks) to designate women in history. I am aware that the contrast Woman/women roughly corresponds to the sex/gender, nature/culture binaries and that I am potentially raising a number of problems in replicating that distinction. I will adhere to this distinction, however, in light of needing to make distinctions between Woman as a male ideal, women as subjects in history or narrative, and the feminine as potentially subversive of the male ideal.

2. On the need to move beyond the fundamental sex/gender distinction within feminist thought, see Tina Chanter *ethics of eros: Irigaray's Rewriting of the Philosophers* (New York: Routledge, 1995), especially ch. 1, "Tracking Essentialism with the Help of a Sex/Gender Map," 21–46.

3. Many feminist authors have examined the dangers of constituting women's identity as exclusive of, or overriding, all others. See, for example, Elizabeth Spelman, *Inessential Woman: Problems of Exclusion in Feminist Thought* (Boston: Beacon Press, 1988); Judith Butler, *Gender Trouble: Feminism and the Subversion of Identity* (New York: Routledge, 1990); Denise Riley, *"Am I That Name?"*; and bell hooks, *"Ain't I a Woman?" Black Women and Feminism* (Boston: South End Press, 1981).

4. See Carol Gilligan, *In a Different Voice* (Cambridge: Harvard University Press, 1982); Sara Ruddick, *Maternal Thinking: Toward a Politics of Peace* (New York: Ballantine, 1989); Jean Bethke Elshtain, *Public Man, Private Woman* (Princeton: Princeton University Press, 1981); and Joan Tronto, *Moral Boundaries: A Political Argument for an Ethic of Care* (New York: Routledge, 1993).

5. Feminist theorists such as Carole Pateman, Madelyn Gutwirth, and Joan Landes have persuasively argued that the modern political sphere, the founding of the social contract, was constructed as inclusive solely of citizen man. Woman was not simply left out of the equation, but rather directly and deliberately excluded in order to define both the physical space of the public sphere and the psychic condition of manhood. See Carole Pateman, *The Sexual Contract* (Stanford: Stanford University Press, 1988); Madelyn Gutwirth, *The Twilight of the Goddesses: Women and Representation in the French Revolutionary Era* (New Brunswick, N.J.: Rutgers University Press, 1992); and Joan Landes, *Women in the Public Sphere in the Age of the French Revolution* (Ithaca: Cornell University Press, 1988). In contrast, Dena Goodman has argued that rhetoric against women to the contrary, women played a central role in creating public space for the intellectual conversation defining Enlightenment thought and practice. See Goodman's work on the *salonnières* in *The Republic of Letters: A Cultural History of the French Enlightenment* (Ithaca: Cornell University Press, 1994). For analyses of women's relationship to citizenship during the revolutionary period that seek to relate women's dilemma to contemporary feminist debates, see Geneviève Fraisse, *Reason's Muse: Sexual Difference and the Birth of Democracy* (Chicago: University of Chicago Press, 1994) and Joan Wallach Scott, *Only Paradoxes to Offer: French Feminists and the Rights of Man* (Cambridge: Harvard University Press, 1996).

6. A comprehensive listing of the literature discussing women's relationship to citizenship, especially as mapped in critiques of the history of Western philosophy would fill pages. As a sample of the discussion of how citizen is consistently gendered as male, see Susan Okin, *Women in Western Political Thought* (Princeton: Princeton University Press, 1979); Elshtain, *Public Man, Private Woman;* Genevieve Lloyd, *The Man of Reason: "Male" and "Female" in Western Philosophy* (Minneapolis: University of Minnesota Press, 1984); Wendy Brown, *Manhood and Politics: A Feminist Reading in Political Theory* (Totawa, N.J.: Rowman and Littlefield, 1988); Landes, *Women in the Public Sphere;* Pateman, *The Sexual Contract* and *The Disorder of Women* (Stanford: Stanford University Press, 1989); Iris Marion Young, *Justice and the Politics of*

Difference (Princeton: Princeton University Press, 1990); Christine Di Stefano, *Configurations of Masculinity: A Feminist Perspective on Modern Political Theory* (Ithaca: Cornell University Press, 1991); and Linda M. G. Zerilli, *Signifying Woman: Culture and Chaos in Rousseau, Burke, and Mill* (Ithaca: Cornell University Press, 1994).

7. My work would not be possible were it not for feminist scholarship that, in response to women's exclusion from the categories of individual and citizen, has scrutinized the constructions of these very categories. Linda M. G. Zerilli, for instance, has argued that Woman is not an "embodied social referent," but rather an "essentially contested concept." "Woman is neither outside the margins nor at the margins of the political; instead, she constitutes and unsettles those margins" (*Signifying Women*, 2).

8. The idea of a *supplément* is Jacques Derrida's from *On Grammatology*, trans. Gayatri Chakravorty Spivak (Baltimore: Johns Hopkins University Press, 1976), 156–57. Here Derrida speaks of Thérèse as supplement for Jean-Jacques—in other words, as necessary to create his identity, yet quickly denied or maybe forgotten. What Derrida calls the "immediate presence" or in Rousseau's system a "metaphysics of presence" is created through an infinite chain of supplements—in Derrida's reading of the *Confessions*, he notes that Mamma is the supplement for an unknown mother, that Thérèse is the supplement for Mamma: "That all begins through the intermediary [woman] is what is indeed 'inconceivable [to reason].'"

9. Scott, *Only Paradoxes to Offer*, 11.

10. I will speak directly to this question in Chapter 2.

11. Pateman, *The Sexual Contract*.

12. Carol Blum, *Rousseau and the Republic of Virtue: The Language of Politics in the French Revolution* (Ithaca: Cornell University Press, 1986).

13. See, for example, Susan Okin, *Women in Western Political Thought*, especially ch. 8, "The Fate of Rousseau's Heroines." For conflicting views on the effects of Rousseau's gender boundaries for women's equality, see Joel Schwartz, *The Sexual Politics of Jean-Jacques Rousseau* (Chicago: University of Chicago Press, 1984), who argues that Rousseau desires a complementary rather than a hierarchical relationship between the sexes, as opposed to Penny A. Weiss, *Gendered Community: Rousseau, Sex, and Politics* (New York: New York University Press, 1993), who argues that Rousseau's gendered education fails to produce any semblance of equality for women.

14. To be fair to Susan Okin's argument in *Women in Western Political Thought*, I must note that she does not think that Rousseau is satisfied with the necessity of his heroines' deaths or the fate of his male characters either. Where I differ from Okin is in my attention to Rousseau's women at the level that we take seriously their actions and words as an alternative that lies at the core of Rousseau's democratic theory and undermines his prescriptions for a nationalistic republic.

15. There is one important exception to this absence. Juliet Flower MacCannell, *The Regime of the Brother: After the Patriarchy* (New York: Routledge, 1991), has deftly explored the "feminine" aspects of Rousseau's *Confessions* and *La Nouvelle Héloïse*, but she does not expand on the political implications of the feminine presence. I will refer to her work throughout this book where relevant.

16. Anne A. A. Mini, "Reconstructing a Past in the Image of the Future: Mme de Staël's Reconception of French Revolutionary Identity," presented at the 1994 Annual Meeting of the Western Political Science Association, Albuquerque, New Mexico, March 10–12, 1994.

17. Debates between liberals and communitarians dominate the discourse about citizenship, and neither camp is particularly concerned about gender politics. Liberals value a rational conception of human liberty, blithely advancing the male as human; communitarians regularly assert a common interest without fully considering groups or individuals who might be excluded on the basis of cultural difference, histories of oppression, voluntary disassociation, and the like. Women are forced to choose between a conception of liberal male citizenship and of republican common good. The problems of the liberal model are clear: women must become like men to be treated as citizens. The problems of the republican model are twofold: the good might be formulated in a male-dominated civic republican tradition that excludes women from politics or in a difference-oriented feminist conception that tends to assume an essential nature of woman. Because the notion of community has historically excluded women, they have often based claims to inclusion on gendered virtue; that is, women's maternal and wifely contributions to society. For an example of the most theoretically developed version of the liberal model of citizenship, see John Rawls, *A Theory of Justice* (Oxford: Oxford University Press, 1971) and *Political Liberalism* (New York: Columbia University Press, 1993); for the communitarian position (with a variety of stances *within* this camp), see Charles Taylor, *Philosophy and the Human Sciences*, Philosophical Papers 2 (Cambridge: Cambridge University Press, 1985); Alasdair MacIntyre, *After*

Virtue (Notre Dame: Notre Dame University Press, 1984); Michael Sandel, *Liberalism and the Limits of Justice* (Cambridge: Cambridge University Press, 1982); and Michael Walzer, *Spheres of Justice* (New York: Basic Books, 1983).

18. Part of the reason contemporary feminists have been left to grapple with the dichotomy between claiming equality with men (via the liberal model) and positing women's difference and superiority (via the communitarian model) is contained within the way the category of *citizen* has been advanced in the history of Western philosophy. This citizen is a straw man: he is completely rational, coldly detached, utterly objective, and either keenly self-interested or surprisingly able to put the public good above his own interest. This "man of reason" (Lloyd, *Man of Reason*) is able to suppress his passion, deny his desire, control his bodily appetites. With these characteristics defining the citizen man, private woman tends to take on mirror opposite characteristics. Though feminist scholars note that neither masculine nor feminine categories have any basis in "nature" but are rather social constructions, with citizen man looking so rational, citizen woman tends to look like his mirror opposite—emotional, passionate, deriving her knowledge from familial interaction. For an introduction to this debate, see Gisela Bock and Susan James, eds., *Beyond Equality and Difference: Citizenship, Feminist Politics and Female Subjectivity* (New York: Routledge, 1992).

19. I will discuss this in Chapters 4 and 5 with regard to why Staël thought extraordinary women, in particular, were often targeted for repression. Since artistic and political women challenged social norms for proper behavior, the power and force of public opinion often stifled their talent. Clearly, Staël sees herself as victim to this phenomenon; she also discusses the fate of Marie-Antoinette in this light.

20. Staël, *On the Influence of the Passions on the Happiness of Individuals and Nations* (1796), in *Oeuvres Completes de Madame de Staël* (London: Baldwin, Cradock and Joy, 1818), III:288–89. Anne A. A. Mini translates this quote in "An Expressive Revolution: The Political Theory of Germaine de Staël," Ph.D. diss., University of Washington, 1995, p. 202.

21. Most notably, as part of my discussion of both Rousseau and Staël, I will address the dangers of advancing pity as a political principle against which Hannah Arendt warned in *On Revolution* (New York: Viking Press, 1963).

22. For an analysis of the ways individual stories of marginalized citizens challenge the basic tenets of Enlightenment thought, see Lori Jo Marso, "The

Stories of Citizens: Rousseau, Montesquieu, and de Staël challenge Enlightenment Reason," *Polity* 30, no. 3 (Spring 1998): 435–63.

23. Lisa J. Disch, "More Truth Than Fact: Storytelling as Critical Understanding in the Writings of Hannah Arendt," *Political Theory* 21, no. 4 (November 1993): 665–94 at p. 665.

24. Aristotle, *Nicomachean Ethics*, Book Six: 7, trans. Terence Irwin (Indianapolis: Hackett, 1985), 158, my emphasis.

25. Nussbaum, *The Fragility of Goodness*, 186–87.

26. Sarah Kofman, "Rousseau's Phallocratic Ends," in *Revaluing French Feminism*, ed. Nancy Fraser and Sandra Lee Bartky (Bloomington: Indiana University Press, 1992), 48.

27. Okin, *Women in Western Political Thought*, 149.

28. Gayle Rubin, "The Traffic in Women: Notes on the 'Political Economy' of Sex," In *Toward an Anthropology of Women*, ed. R. R. Reiter (New York: Monthly Review Press, 1975), 174.

29. Arendt, *On Revolution*, 81.

30. Ibid.

31. Goodman, *The Republic of Letters*, 83.

32. Ibid., 82.

33. Much of the literature that reads Staël as a woman who really wants to be a man derives from the "definitive" but antifeminist biography of Staël: J. Christopher Herold, *Mistress to an Age: A Life of Madame de Staël* (New York: Bobbs-Merrill Co., 1959).

34. See Madelyn Gutwirth "Marie-Antoinette, Scourge of the French People," in *Twilight of the Goddesses*, 228–45; Elizabeth Colwill, "Just Another Citoyenne? Marie-Antoinette on Trial, 1790–1793," *History Workshop* 28 (Autumn 1989): 63–87; and Lynn Hunt, "The Many Bodies of Marie-Antoinette: Political Pornography and the Problem of the Feminine in the French Revolution," in *Eroticism and the Body Politic*, ed. Lynn Hunt (Baltimore: Johns Hopkins University Press, 1991), 108–30.

35. Luce Iragaray, "The Blind Spot of an Old Dream of Symmetry," in *Speculum of the Other Woman* (Ithaca: Cornell University Press, 1985), 84.

36. Luce Iragaray, *This Sex Which Is Not One*, trans. Catherine Porter (Ithaca: Cornell University Press, 1985), 27.

CHAPTER 2
(Re)examining the Feminine Presence
Rousseau's Sophie

1. Tracy Strong, *Jean-Jacques Rousseau: The Politics of the Ordinary* (Thousand Oaks, Calif.: Sage, 1994).

2. Weiss, *Gendered Community*, 121.

3. Young, *Justice and the Politics of Difference*, 229.

4. Within the literature that praises Rousseau for his ability to create a good and moral community, when gender is addressed at all, men and women's roles are seen as complementary. See, for example, Schwartz, *Sexual Politics of Rousseau* (1984) on the equal, though different, powers of the sexes. Feminist critiques of Rousseau are too numerous to list. I address a number of them throughout.

5. Zerilli, *Signifying Women*, 18.

6. Elizabeth Wingrove, "Sexual Performance as Political Performance in the *Lettre À M. D'Alembert Sur Les Spectacles,*" *Political Theory* 23, no. 4 (November 1995): 585–616 at p. 587.

7. Weiss, *Gendered Community*, 37.

8. Okin, *Women in Western Political Thought*, 132.

9. Mary Wollstonecraft, *Vindication of the Rights of Woman*, ed. Carol H. Poston (New York: W. W. Norton, 1988), 42.

10. Elshtain, *Public Man, Private Woman*, 159.

11. The most recent version of this interpretation of Rousseau appears in Joan Wallach Scott's *Only Paradoxes to Offer:*

> For Rousseau, the way finally to manage, if not to eliminate, the dangers of erotic excess in both sexes was to restrain it in women. Thus Sophie's education aims at making her a modest, selfless creature whose only goal is to serve her husband; her job is to confirm Emile in his vision of himself, not to seek through him a self of her own. The key to her education lies in the control if not the repression of her imagination. (28)

12. Strong, *Jean-Jacques Rousseau*, 84.

13. Ibid., 54.

14. Arendt, *On Revolution*, 83; my emphasis.

15. Young, *Justice and the Politics of Difference*, 233.

16. Richard Sennett, *The Fall of Public Man* (New York: Vintage, 1974), 115.

17. Young, *Justine and the Politics of Difference*, 231.

18. Ibid., 238.

19. Goodman, *The Republic of Letters*, 74.

20. Judith Sklar, *Men and Citizens* (Cambridge: Cambridge University Press, 1969), 235.

21. Marshall Berman, *The Politics of Authenticity: Radical Individualism and the Emergence of Modern Society* (New York: Antheneum, 1972), and Alessandro Ferrara, *Modernity and Authenticity: A Study of the Social and Ethical Thought of Jean-Jacques Rousseau* (Albany: State University of New York Press, 1993).

CHAPTER 3
The Dangerous Insider
Rousseau's Julie

1. Peggy Kamuf, *Fictions of Feminine Desire: Disclosures of Heloise* (Lincoln: University of Nebraska Press, 1982), 97.

2. Ferrara, *Modernity and Authenticity*, 93.

3. Ibid., 105.

4. Ibid., 106.

5. Lisa Disch, "Claire Loves Julie: Reading the Story of Women's Friendship in *La Nouvelle Héloïse*," *Hypatia: A Journal of Feminist Philosophy* 9, no. 3 (Summer 1994): 19–45. Long before this essay was published in *Hypatia*, I was a member of a panel at the 1991 Midwest Political Science Association Conference at which Disch presented an earlier version of this essay. Her interpretation of Rousseau, and of this novel specifically, both complemented and deeply informed my own work on Rousseau.

6. Kamuf, *Fictions of Feminine Desire*, 121–22.

7. MacCannell, *Regime of the Brother*, 87–89.

8. Zerilli, *Signifying Women*, 44–45.

9. This translation is taken from Judith McDowell, *Julie, or the New Eloise* (University Park: Penn State University Press, 1968), II:XV, 198.

10. Carol Blum, *Rousseau and the Republic of Virtue,* notes that Rousseau reveals in *Confessions* that, in his later years, masturbation came to replace all sexual activity for him. This isolation was very much part of Rousseau's other self-absorbed ways. Blum writes:

> With himself as sexual partner, Rousseau wrote of turning to his own fantasies for sensual pleasure, withdrawing from the real world and plunging into his own mind to maintain the feelings of virtue which he called necessary to his well-being. In his youth, some twenty-five years before, when he was living as the protégé of Mme. de Warens, his masturbation had been so obvious that she, alarmed at his habits, took him to her bed. He reacted to this change in their relationship with an "invincible sadness which poisoned the charm." His [Rousseau's] autobiographical writings place the origins of the problem of whether it was better to masturbate or to enter into a real affair with a woman during those years. (59)

11. Jean Starobinski, *Jean-Jacques Rousseau: Transparency and Obstruction,* trans. Arthur Goldhammer (Chicago: University of Chicago Press, 1988), 99.

12. Schwartz, *Sexual Politics of Rousseau,* 125.

13. Disch, "Claire Loves Julie," 37.

14. Ibid., 38.

15. Schwartz, *Sexual Politics of Rousseau,* 7.

16. Ibid., 115.

17. Victoria Wohl, "Exchange, Gender, and Subjectivity," in *Too Intimate Commerce* (Austin: University of Texas Press, 1998), xiii.

18. Luce Irigaray, *This Sex Which Is Not One,* 27.

19. Susan Bickford, "Why We Listen to Lunatics: Antifoundational Theories and Feminist Politics," *Hypatia* 8, no. 2 (Spring 1993): 114.

20. Michel Foucault, "Is It Useless to Revolt?" *Philosophy and Social Criticism* 8, no. 1, (1981): 3–9, quoted in Bickford, "Why We Listen to Lunatics," 15.

21. Unless, of course, we concur with Joel Schwartz in his observation that women's passive and indirect citizenship (their contribution to the private sphere) is considered just as important and highly valued as men's public and active citizenship.

22. Wendy Farley, *Eros for the Other: Retaining Truth in a Pluralistic World* (University Park: Penn State University Press, 1996), 50.

23. Baudelaire, "The Eyes of the Poor," in *Paris Spleen* (New York: New Directions, 1970), 52.

24. Ibid., 52.

25. Ibid., 53.

26. Marshall Berman, *All That Is Solid Melts Into Air: The Experience of Modernity* (New York: Penguin, 1988), 148–55.

CHAPTER 4

The Loving Citizen

Staël's Delphine

1. Staël notes a conversation in 1797, before Bonaparte's ascent to power, between Napoleon Bonaparte and "a French lady distinguished for her beauty, her wit, and the ardour of her opinions: [Bonaparte] placed himself straight before her, like the stiffest of the German generals, and said to her, 'Madam, I don't like women to meddle with politics.' 'You are right, General,' replied she; 'but in a country where they lose their heads, it is natural for them to desire to know the reason'" (CFR, III:II:XXVI, 201). Staël later notes that she was the "first woman whom Bonaparte exiled; but a great number, adherents of opposite opinion, soon shared [her] fate." Staël argues that Bonaparte had "a hatred against all independent beings," especially women, and notes that she was probably exiled because she was the "only writer of reputation in France, who had published books during his reign without making any mention of his gigantic existence" (CFR, II:IV:VIII, 302–33).

2. Staël herself narrowly escaped the scaffold thirteen months earlier. She vividly relates the narrative of her hasty departure from Paris on 2 September 1792 (CFR, II:III:X, 72–74). It is interesting to note that she frequently refers to her sex in recounting her own reasonableness (and love of liberty) and in noting the lack of sympathy in her accusers.

3. Colwill, "Just Another *Citoyenne*?" 64.

4. Madelyn Gutwirth, Lynn Hunt, Elizabeth Colwill, and Sarah Maza have documented the significance of the queen's trial and execution for the destiny of women in the revolution and the ways in which the mythology of the queen was constructed to lend legitimacy to the new republic. See Gutwirth's "Marie-Antoinette, Scourge of the French People," in *Twilight of the Goddesses*, 228–38; Hunt's "The Many Bodies of Marie Antoinette"; and Sarah Maza's "The Diamond Necklace Affair Revisited (1785–1786): The Case of

the Missing Queen," in *Eroticism and the Body Politic*, ed. Lynn Hunt (Baltimore: Johns Hopkins University Press, 1991).

5. Joan B. Landes, in *Women and the Public Sphere*, shows that "according to the logic of republican motherhood, woman's major task was to instill her children with patriotic duty . . . and the potential for providing women with a route into the public sphere by way of republican motherhood was undermined by the claims of nature" (138).

6. Madelyn Gutwirth, *Twilight of the Goddesses*, 239, argues that there is a "huge existential gap between the ideology of gender and the in-the-home and on-the-street raw realities of women's actual behavior. . . . Just as we jockey mentally in daily life with insistent ideas of female 'goodness,' 'purity,' and 'beauty' in face of the full range of female 'badness,' 'impurity,' and lack of 'beauty' we encounter," so did women's revolutionary activity and violence challenge the gender roles so prevalent during the Revolution. The reaction to this blurring of gender boundaries was to reinforce the boundaries all the more vigorously. Men feared that women's political action would serve to threaten their own masculinity (and hence, their citizenship). See also Linda M. G. Zerilli's fascinating study of "political theory as a signifying practice" in *Signifying Woman*. Zerilli argues that the foundation of the man or citizen (society and politics) stands on "nothing but [the] quicksand" of sexual difference signified in language. As such, men want women to be women (feminine and domestic) so that they can be men (masculine and public). Men fear women's participation in politics as they fear their own feminization. (See ch. 1, pp. 1–15).

7. As Joan Scott writes: "Feminism's inherently political aspect comes from its critical engagement with prevailing theories and practices; it does not stand as an independent philosophical movement with an autonomous content and a independent legacy of its own" ("A Woman Who Has Only Paradoxes to Offer: Olympe de Gouges Claims Rights for Women," in *Rebel Daughters: Women and the French Revolution*, ed. Sara E. Melzer and Leslie W. Rabine [New York: Oxford University Press, 1992], 106.)

8. Kathleen B. Jones, "Citizenship in a Woman-Friendly Polity," *Signs* 15, no. 4 (Summer 1990): 792.

9. "Shameless prostitutes, slaves degraded by their fate, women secluded in their homes and unknown to the rest of the world, strangers to the concerns of their husbands, reared to have neither ideas nor feelings—this is all the Greeks knew of ties of love" (OLB, I:I, 157).

10. Hearing a famous minstrel sing the painful story of the Greek return from Troy, Penelope begs her son Telemachus to make him stop and sing something else: that particular verse is too vivid a reminder of the one she loved and lost, and the memory is too agonizing to bear. The son dismisses his mother's request as too personal, too emotional, too bound to the ties of love. According to Telemachus:

> Courage, mother. Harden your heart, and listen.
> But you must nerve yourself and try to listen.
> Odysseus was scarcely the only one, you know,
> whose journey home was blotted out at Troy.
> Others, so many others, died there too.

> (Homer, *The Odyssey*, trans. Robert Fagles
> [New York: Penguin, 1996] Bk. I, p. 89)

Rebuffed, Penelope returns to her room to cry. Telemachus, newly ordained into the world of men, shows pleasure in admonishing his mother, naming his father as one among many dead, and diminishing the centrality and relevance of emotion and the ties of love in the highly masculine forum of war and politics. This passage is discussed by Lawrence Lipking, "Aristotle's Sister: A Poetics of Abandonment," *Critical Inquiry* 10 (1983–84): 65.

11. Friedrich Nietzsche, *The Gay Science*, trans. Walter Kaufmann (New York: Vintage, 1974), 262. Quoted by Melissa A. Orlie, "Thoughtless Assertion and Political Deliberation," *American Political Science Review* 88, no. 3 (September 1994): 692. In this article Orlie makes a fascinating argument for "political perspectivism" based in a reading of Nietzsche and Arendt. Orlie convincingly argues that we can create a plural political space by recognizing the "distinctness of our bodies" in political spaces, "open[ing] ourselves to others' perspectives with a willingness to transfigure 'who' we are becoming."

12. "Opinion is the grave of virtue among men and its throne among women" (E, V:365).

13. Benhabib, *Situating the Self*, 6, argues that searching for these disjunctions corresponds to the *moral* point of view in the stages of reasoning.

14. Neither liberalism nor communitarianism are monolithic terms. When I speak of each, I am referring solely to general tendencies within which there are a variety of different, sometimes conflicting positions. For the purposes of the stated opposition between the two (liberalism and communitarianism), however, I find it is sufficient to treat each position in a general manner.

15. Strong, *Jean-Jacques Rousseau*, 74.

16. Ibid., 31. Strong argues that Rousseau desires a common will that would allow people to experience what is most human (common or ordinary) in themselves and others, that is, the ability to "experience society as life with others and with oneself" (34). I will argue that Staël desires the kind of politics that conforms to Strong's interpretation of the Rousseauian model in that she argues that a good citizen is able to recognize commonality *as well as* difference. In contrast to Strong, however, I maintain that in *banishing* women from politics and requiring that one abstract from the particular in debating and deciding on the requirements of the *general* will, Rousseau denies his own desire to maintain multiplicity by giving priority to the ordinary. The move to define morality as prior and superior to emotions/passions/Eros, which Kant adopts in his definition of a priori reason, is intricately bound up with the sexual politics of Rousseau's theory.

17. Madelyn Gutwirth, *Germaine de Staël: The Emergence of the Artist as a Woman* (Urbana: University of Illinois Press, 1978) argues that Delphine is trapped by conceptions of traditional femininity. She lives as fully as she can as a woman, yet her exceptional qualities serve to deny her the fulfillment of marriage and family. Gutwirth's pioneering work on Staël has inspired many subsequent feminist studies of Staël, including my own.

18. D, I:2, 13. Though Delphine needs a partner with whom to share her life politically and emotionally, being a woman with superior qualities and an independent character will prevent the fulfillment of her desires. Jean Starobinski argues that for Staël, exceptional qualities lead to a sense of incompleteness. She will long for another in quest for wholeness, and when love fails, enter a phase of living death ("Suicide et melancolie chez Mme de Staël," *Preuves* 190, no. 16 [1966]: 41–48). Staël's novel *Delphine* is in one sense a testimony to this living death. Vivian Folkenflik, *An Extraordinary Woman: Selected Writings of Germaine de Staël* (New York: Columbia University Press, 1987) notes that "both independence and connectedness are essential to her [Delphine's] being" (24).

19. "The men and women who were conducted to the scaffold gave proofs of a courage that nothing could shake; the prisons presented the example of the most generous acts of devotion; fathers were seen sacrificing themselves for their sons, wives for their husbands; but the party of the worthy, like the King himself, showed themselves capable only of private virtues" (CFR, II:III: XIX, 139).

20. Colwill, "Just Another *Citoyenne?*" 76.

21. Tronto, *Moral Boundaries*, 2.

22. Hunt, "The Many Bodies of Marie-Antoinette," 123.

23. Mini, "An Expressive Revolution," 234.

24. Farley, *Eros for the Other*, 156.

25. Rawls, *A Theory of Justice*.

26. Blum, *Rousseau and the Republic of Virtue*.

27. Bonnie Honig, *Political Theory and the Displacement of Politics* (Ithaca: Cornell University Press, 1993).

28. As described by Staël, the good citizen subscribes to Seyla Benhabib's recommendation that moral and political deliberation be conducted according to the model of "interactive universalism" ("The Generalized and Concrete Other: The Kohlberg-Gilligan Controversy and Moral Theory," in *Situating the Self*, 165).

29. Benhabib, *Situating the Self*, 159. See also Tronto, *Moral Boundaries*. Benhabib introduces Hannah Arendt's vision of "enlarged mentality" to argue for a model of political morality in which one takes the standpoint of the concrete other into account when deliberating moral questions. Tronto opposes her vision of *contextual* morality (rooted in Aristotelian ethics) to Kantian morality in order to advance an ethic of care separate from the political context, which has construed morality as inherently gendered. In Staël's compelling detail of individual lives and the effects of politics on these lives, she convinces us that politics *cannot* be adequately theorized in abstraction. Staël exclaims: "Atrocious men thought they could simplify their calculations [of politics] by omitting suffering, feeling, and imagination; they had no conception of the nature of general truths. These truths are made up of *every fact* and *every individual being*" (OLB, 247, emphasis added).

30. Arendt, *On Revolution*, 85–86.

31. Benhabib, "Judgment and Politics in Arendt's Thought," *Situating the Self*, 137.

32. My use of this phrase is inspired by J. Peter Euben's article "Antigone and the Languages of Politics," in *Corrupting Youth: Political Education, Democratic Culture, and Political Theory* (Princeton: Princeton University Press, 1997).

33. Ibid., 160.

34. Lynn Hunt, "The Unstable Boundaries of the French Revolution," *A History of Private Life* (Cambridge: Belknap Press of Harvard University Press, 1990), IV:13–45. See also Blum, *Rousseau and the Republic of Virtue.*

35. Statement of the Temporary Commission of Republican Vigilance Established in "Emancipated City" (Lyons), November 1793, quoted in Hunt, "Unstable Boundaries," 15.

36. Robespierre, 5 February, 1794, quoted in Hunt, "Unstable Boundaries," 14.

37. This point is made convincingly by Mary Jacobus, "Incorruptible Milk: Breast-feeding and the French Revolution," in *Rebel Daughters: Women and the French Revolution,* ed. Sara E. Melzer and Leslie W. Rabine (New York: Oxford University Press, 1992).

38. Hunt, "Unstable Boundaries," 8.

39. Jacobus, "Incorruptible Milk," 65.

40. In fact, this is precisely what the revolutionaries most feared. In a chapter entitled "The Maenad Factor; or Sex, Politics, and Murderousness," in *Twilight of the Goddesses,* 307–40, Madelyn Gutwirth notes that female sexual rage became the metaphor for the Revolution in playing upon male fear that women's political action would usurp their own masculinity.

CHAPTER 5

Theorizing Women's Desire
Staël's Corinne

1. One who improvises poetry. The role is usually associated with a woman who plays the harp while reciting whatever inspiration brings to mind concerning the theme given by herself or suggested by the audience.

2. "Her last name was not known; her first work had come out five years earlier signed only *Corinne.* No one knew where she had lived before or what kind of person she had been" (CI, II:I, 20).

3. This theme has been fruitfully explored by Anne A. A. Mini in terms of Staël's desire to create a new national identity for France that would not break with its cultural heritage. See Mini, "Reconstructing a Past."

4. Scott, *Only Paradoxes to Offer,* 23.

5. Ibid., 21.

6. Ibid., 25–27.

7. Ibid., 28.

8. Luce Irigaray, *Speculum of the Other Woman*, 89 n. 92.

9. Staël calls attention to Corinne as an improvisatrice with an entirely original way of using language. I am convinced, however, that Staël does not seek to identify Corinne's language as essentially feminine. Instead it is something new, unable to be captured by traditional ways of naming. In this I think Staël's project also prefigures Julia Kristeva's theory of female subjectivity. In her famous essay, "Women's Time," Kristeva states that "the very dichotomy man/woman as an opposition between two rival entities may be understood as belonging to metaphysics. What can 'identity,' even 'sexual identity,' mean in a new theoretical and scientific space where the very notion of identity is challenged?" (in *The Kristeva Reader*, ed. Toril Moi [New York: Columbia University Press, 1986], 209).

10. Plato, *The Republic*, trans. G. M. A. Grube (Indianapolis, Ind.: Hackett, 1992), Bk. X, 273. References hereafter are to this edition.

11. Irigaray, "The Power of Discourse," in *This Sex Which Is Not One*, 76.

12. Geneviève Fraisse, *Reason's Muse: Sexual Difference and the Birth of Democracy* (Chicago: University of Chicago Press, 1994), 103.

13. I owe this initial point and the use of the term *gaze* to describe Oswald's male sight of Corinne to Nancy K. Miller, "Performances of the Gaze: Staël's *Corinne, or Italy*," in *Subject to Change: Reading Feminist Writing* (New York: Columbia University Press, 1988), 162–203. In this compelling reading of *Corinne*, Miller argues, via John Berger, that men do not simply look; their gaze carries with it the power of action and of possession that is lacking in the female gaze. Miller sees a battle going on in the text between the judgments of patriarchy (Oswald) and the desires of a feminine subject (Corinne).

14. Margaret H. Darrow, "French Noblewomen and the New Domesticity," *Feminist Studies* 5, no. 1 (1979): 58.

15. For this insight I thank Bertell Ollman, who pointed this out to me the first time he read the manuscript.

16. Scott, *Only Paradoxes to Offer*, x–xi.

17. Jane Flax, "Beyond Equality: Gender, Justice and Difference," in *Beyond Equality and Difference: citizenship, feminist politics, female subjectivity*, ed. Gisela Bock and Susan James (New York: Routledge, 1992), 193–210 at pp. 193–94.

18. Kathleen B. Jones, "Citizenship in a Woman-Friendly Polity," 781–812, quoting Virginia Sapiro, "When are Interests Interesting? The Problem of Political Representation of Women," *American Political Science Review* 75 (September 1981): 717–21.

19. Landes, *Women in the Public Sphere*, 12.

20. Charlotte Hogsett, *The Literary Existence of Germaine de Staël* (Carbondale: Southern Illinois University Press, 1987), 111–12 (emphasis added). Hogsett convincingly details how in *Corinne* love not only does not win out, but it also destroys Corinne in the process:

> At the beginning of the book, Corinne is honored on the Capitoline hill. She receives a Petrarchan crown and then improvises before an adoring crowd. Her talents, combined with her exposure to two quite different cultures, have given her special powers of creativity. . . . Corinne's crown falls when she sees Oswald for the first time. Later in the novel she crowns him for a heroic act he has performed. Still later, in a moment of intense suffering over their lost love, she falls down, hitting and cutting her head. She bitterly points out that a crown once adorned this now bleeding head.

Hogsett attributes this loss of creativity to the inability of the artist to "participate in a strongly centralized, integrated oneness with another." In this sense, she says, love "is structured like totalitarian governments."

I disagree with this interpretation of Hogsett's, which follows on Madelyn Gutwirth's isolation of Corinne's statement that "talent requires an inner independence true love does not permit." It is true that Corinne's talent flourished before she met Oswald and that it deteriorates in the course of their relationship. However, Corinne is anxious to love; she does not want to pursue her talent at the expense of love; she wants to integrate these two aspects of her personality. It is Oswald who, despite his love for Corinne, will not allow the integration because of an ingrained norm for women. When he loves Corinne *as herself*, her ability to perform is enhanced.

21. It would be ridiculous to think that Staël was a writer and actor outside politics. All of her works are clearly political. *Delphine*, a novel that Staël says was to focus on private emotions and love, does do precisely that. But in Staël's framework, a focus on love is *political*. See Susan Tenenbaum, "The Coppet Circle: Literary Criticism as Political Discourse," *History of Political Thought* 1, no. 3 (1980): 453–73, for a fascinating discussion on the interrelationship of politics and culture in Staël's salon in Coppet from 1804 to 1810.

22. In *Delphine*, for instance, the social structure is responsible for women's behavior, petty or otherwise, because of women's destiny for unhappiness within that structure. However, the social structure also creates a potential for moral behavior in women that Staël does not identify in men. Because women are excluded from political life, they have developed a reliance on emotions, private experience, and love—qualities that, according to Staël, should play a role in politics. And in *Corinne, or Italy*, Staël is keen to make the point that the kind of virtue ascribed to women does not come from their biological sex, but rather from the way women have learned to pay attention to detail, particularly emotions of the "concrete other." Speaking of Lady Edgermond, who is clearly not very admirable, Staël writes: "Not losing sight of Oswald for a moment, she [Lady Edgermond] penetrated the secrets of his soul with the insight attributed to women's minds, although it derives solely from the constant observation inspired by true feeling" (CI, XIX:I, 377).

23. It is important to note, though, that Staël does not think emotion should be the sole basis of public morality. In her treatise *On the Influence of the Passions on the Happiness of Individuals and Nations*, Staël clearly makes a case *for* emotion while maintaining that *reason* is needed for universal application of emotion. When Corinne is too heavily swayed by the force of passion, she is unable to write decent prose or improvise in a way that can touch the souls of all: "Unable to divert her thoughts from her own plight, she portrayed her suffering. But no longer were there any general ideas or the universal feelings that correspond to all men's hearts; it was the cry of grief, ultimately monotonous as the cry of birds in the night, too fervent in expression, too vehement, too lacking in subtlety: unhappiness it was, but it was not talent" (CI, XVIII:IV, 368).

24. In his *Mistress to an Age*, Christopher Herold reports: "The official press reacted as was to be expected, denouncing the book as anti-French, . . . Napoleon leafed through it and called it junk" (344). In the Introduction to her translation of *Corinne*, Avriel Goldberger comments that Napoleon may have been as sensitive to what the book omitted as to what it said. She notes that "nowhere are the emperor or his victories mentioned . . . nowhere are the French armies seen" (CI, Intro., xxxii).

25. In her *Considerations on the Principle Events of the French Revolution*, Staël admonishes Napoleon for correcting diversities of opinion like "faults in discipline" (CFR, II:IV:II, 241).

26. This phrase is Susan Tenenbaum's in "Corinne: Political Polemics and the

Theory of the Novel," a soon-to-be published paper in an interdisciplinary collection specifically addressing *Corinne, or Italy*. I will argue that this notion of civic consciousness is represented by Oswald's ties to English liberalism. Staël does not wish to replace English duty with Italian spirit; she looks toward a culture/society/politics that does not opt for one over the other.

27. Staël clearly suspects Napoleon of misogyny: "I was the first woman Napoleon exiled, but he soon banished many others of various opinions. Since women, on the one hand, could in no way further his political schemes, and since, on the other hand, they were less susceptible than men to the fears and hopes that power dispensed, they irritated him like so many rebels, and he took pleasure in saying offensive and vulgar things to them" (Morroe Berger, *Madame de Staël on Politics, Literature, and National Character* [Garden City, N.Y.: Doubleday, 1964], 104–5).

28. According to English Showalter Jr., Corinne "is the first such heroine of any significance. The well-known female characters of eighteenth-century novels all faced primarily the problem of negotiating some sort of self-realization through a compromise with a paternal figure or his surrogate" ("Corinne as an Autonomous Heroine," *Germaine de Staël: Crossing the Borders*, ed. Madelyn Gutwirth, Avriel Goldberger, and Karyna Szmurlo [New Brunswick, N.J.: Rutgers University Press, 1991], 188–92.)

29. See Mary Jacobus, "Incorruptible Milk."

30. Susan Tenenbaum, "Liberal Heroines: Mme de Staël on the <<woman question>> and the modern state," *Annales Benjamin Constant* 5 (1985): 37–52, 46. Tenenbaum argues that Staël felt society had need of both the ordinary Lucile-type, and the extraordinary Corinne-type, women. I argue, in contrast, that Corinne's challenge to the revolution's ideology of woman explodes those traditional boundaries.

CHAPTER 6
Conclusion
Recognizing Women

1. Martha Nussbaum, *Love's Knowledge: Essays on Philosophy and Literature* (New York: Oxford University Press, 1990), 11–12.

2. Du Bois, *Sappho is Burning*.

3. Iris Marion Young, "Impartiality and the Civic Public: Some Implications of Feminist Critiques of Moral and Political Theory," in *Feminism as Critique*,

edited by Seyla Benhabib and Drucilla Cornell (Minneapolis: University of Minnesota Press), *6*.

4. Zerilli, *Signifying Woman*, 143.

5. MacCannell, *Regime of the Brother*, 123.

6. Drucilla Cornell, *The Imaginary Domain* (New York: Routledge, 1995), 8. Cornell radicalizes and expands on John Rawls' *Theory of Justice* and *Political Liberalism* to develop her notion of the "imaginary domain." Respect for the imaginary domain of each individual allows us to "come to terms with who we are and who we wish to be as sexuate beings" (8). As such, she escapes the dualism between equality and difference in that gender parity is formulated, not in terms of male equality, but rather in terms that allow equality in "one's personhood." This can only be achieved by assuming that all are worthy of happiness as sexual beings, a firm refusal to deny sexual difference. I read Julie's maxim on happiness and the desire to treat persons as ends in themselves, as singular individuals, in a similar way.

REFERENCES

·

Arendt, Hannah. *On Revolution*. New York: Viking Press, 1963.

Aristotle. *Nichomachean Ethics*, Bk. 6. Translated by Terence Irwin. Indianapolis: Hackett, 1985.

Baudelaire, Charles-Pierre. "The Eyes of the Poor." In *Paris Spleen*. New York: New Directions, 1970.

Beauvoir, Simone. *The Second Sex*. Translated by H. M. Parshley. New York: Vintage, 1952.

Benhabib, Seyla. *Situating the Self*. New York: Routledge, 1992.

Berger, Morroe. *Madame de Staël on Politics, Literature, and National Character*. Garden City, N.Y.: Doubleday, 1964.

Berman, Marshall. *All That Is Solid Melts into Air: The Experience of Modernity*. New York: Penguin, 1988

———. *The Politics of Authenticity: Radical Individualism and the Emergence of Modern Society*. New York: Antheneum, 1972.

Bickford, Susan. "Why We Listen to Lunatics: Antifoundational Theories and Feminist Politics." *Hypatia* 8, no. 2 (Spring 1993): 104–23 .

Blum, Carol. *Rousseau and the Republic of Virtue: The Language of Politics in the French Revolution*. Ithaca: Cornell University Press, 1986.

Bock, Gisela, and Susan James, eds. *Beyond Equality and Difference: Citizenship, Feminist Politics and Female Subjectivity*. New York: Routledge, 1992.

Brown, Wendy. *Manhood and Politics: A Feminist Reading in Political Theory*. Totawa, N.J.: Rowman and Littlefield, 1988.

Butler, Judith. *Gender Trouble: Feminism and the Subversion of Identity*. New York: Routledge, 1990.

Charter, Tina. *ethics of eros: Irigaray's Rewriting of the Philosophers*. New York: Routledge, 1995.

Colwill, Elizabeth. "Just Another Citoyenne? Marie-Antoinette on Trial, 1790–1793." *History Workshop* 28 (Autumn 1989): 63–87.

Cornell, Drucilla. *The Imaginary Domain*. New York: Routledge, 1995.

Darrow, Margaret H. "French Noblewomen and the New Domesticity." *Feminist Studies* 5, no. 1 (1979): 58.

Derrida, Jacques. *On Grammatology*. Translated by Gayatri Chakravorty Spivak. Baltimore: Johns Hopkins University Press, 1976.

Disch, Lisa. "Claire Loves Julie: Reading the Story of Women's Friendship in *La Nouvelle Héloïse*." *Hypatia: A Journal of Feminist Philosophy* 9, no. 3 (Summer 1994): 19–45.

———. "More Truth Than Fact: Storytelling as Critical Understanding in the Writings of Hannah Arendt." *Political Theory* 21, no. 4 (November 1993): 665–94.

Di Stefano, Christine. *Configurations of Masculinity: A Feminist Perspective on Modern Political Theory*. Ithaca: Cornell University Press.

Du Bois, Page. *Sappho is Burning*. Chicago: University of Chicago Press, 1995.

Elshtain, Jean Bethke. *Public Man, Private Woman: Women in Social and Political Thought*. Princeton: Princeton University Press, 1981).

Euben, J. Peter. "Antigone and the Languages of Politics." In *Corrupting Youth: Political Education, Democratic Culture, and Political Theory*. Princeton: Princeton University Press, 1997.

Farley, Wendy. *Eros for the Other: Retaining Truth in a Pluralistic World*. University Park: Pennsylvania State University Press, 1996.

Ferrara, Alessandro. *Modernity and Authenticity: A Study of the Social and Ethical Thought of Jean-Jacques Rousseau*. Albany: State University of New York Press, 1993.

Flax, Jane. "Beyond Equality: Gender, Justice and Difference." In *Beyond Equality and Difference: Citizenship, Feminist Politics, Female Subjectivity*. Edited by Gisela Bock and Susan James, 193–210. New York: Routledge, 1992.

Folkenflik, Vivian. *An Extraordinary Woman: Selected Writings of Germaine de Staël*. New York: Columbia University Press, 1987.

Foucault, Michel. "Is It Useless to Revolt?" *Philosophy and Social Criticism* 8, no. 1 (1988): 3–9.

Fraisse, Geneviève. *Reason's Muse: Sexual Difference and the Birth of Democracy.* Chicago: University of Chicago Press, 1994.

Gilligan, Carol. *In a Different Voice.* Cambridge: Harvard University Press, 1982.

Goodman, Dena. *The Republic of Letters: A Cultural History of the French Enlightenment.* Ithaca: Cornell University Press, 1994.

Gutwirth, Madelyn. *Germaine de Staël: The Emergence of the Artist as a Woman.* Urbana: University of Illinois Press, 1978.

————. *The Twilight of the Goddesses: Women and Representation in the French Revolutionary Era.* New Brunswick, N.J.: Rutgers University Press, 1992.

Hartsock, Nancy. *Money, Sex, and Power: Toward a Feminist Historical Materialism.* Boston: Northeastern University Press, 1985.

Herold, Christopher J. *Mistress to an Age: A Life of Madame de Staël.* Indianapolis: Bobbs-Merrill, 1958.

Hogsett, Charlotte. *The Literary Existence of Germaine de Staël.* Carbondale: Southern Illinois University Press, 1987.

Homer. *The Odyssey*, Bk. I. Translated by Robert Fagles. New York: Penguin, 1996.

Honig, Bonnie. *Political Theory and the Displacement of Politics.* Ithaca: Cornell University Press, 1993.

hooks, bell. *"Ain't I a Woman?" Black Women and Feminism.* Boston: South End Press, 1981.

Hunt, Lynn. "The Many Bodies of Marie-Antoinette: Political Pornography and the Problem of the Feminine in the French Revolution." In *Eroticism and the Body Politic.* Edited by Lynn Hunt, 108–30. Baltimore: Johns Hopkins University Press, 1991.

————. "The Unstable Boundaries of the French Revolution." In *A History of Private Life*, IV:13–45. Cambridge: Belknap Press of Harvard University Press, 1990.

Irigaray, Luce. *This Sex Which Is Not One.* Trans. Catherine Porter. Ithaca: Cornell University Press, 1985.

————. *Speculum of the Other Woman.* Translated by Gillian C. Gill. Ithaca: Cornell University Press, 1985.

Jacobus, Mary. "Incorruptible Milk: Breast-feeding and the French Revolution." In *Rebel Daughters: Women and the French Revolution*. Edited by Sara E. Melzer and Leslie W. Rabine. New York: Oxford University Press, 1992.

Jones, Kathleen B. "Citizenship in a Woman-Friendly Polity." *Signs* 15, no. 4 (Summer 1990): 781–813.

Kamuf, Peggy. *Fictions of Feminine Desire: Disclosures of Heloise*. Lincoln: University of Nebraska Press, 1982.

Kofman, Sarah. "Rousseau's Phallocratic Ends." In *Revaluing French Feminism*. Edited by Nancy Fraser and Sandra Lee Bartky. Bloomington: Indiana University Press, 1992.

Kristeva, Julie. "Women's Time." In *The Kristeva Reader*. Edited by Toril Moi. New York: Columbia University Press, 1986.

Landes, Joan B. *Women and the Public Sphere in the Age of the French Revolution*. Ithaca: Cornell University Press, 1988.

Lipking, Lawrence. "Aristotle's Sister: A Poetics of Abandonment." *Critical Inquiry* 10 (1983–84): 61–81.

Lloyd, Genevieve. *The Man of Reason: "Male" and "Female" in Western Philosophy*. Minneapolis: University of Minnesota Press, 1984.

MacCannell, Juliet Flower. *The Regime of the Brother: After the Patriarchy*. New York: Routledge, 1991.

MacIntyre, Alasdair. *After Virtue*. Notre Dame: University of Notre Dame Press, 1984.

Marso, Lori Jo. "The Loving Citizen: Germaine de Staël's *Delphine*." *Journal of Political Philosophy* 5, no. 2 (June 1997): 109–31.

———. "The Stories of Citizens: Rousseau, Montesquieu, and de Staël Challenge Enlightenment Reason." *Polity* 30, no. 3 (Spring 1998): 435–63.

Maza, Sarah. "The Diamond Necklace Affair Revisited (1785–1786): The Case of the Missing Queen." In *Eroticism and the Body Politic*. Edited by Lynn Hunt. Baltimore: Johns Hopkins University Press, 1991.

McDowell, Judith. *Julie, or the New Eloise*. University Park: Pennsylvania State University Press, 1968.

Miller, Nancy. "Performances of the Gaze: Staël's *Corinne, or Italy*." In *Subject to Change: Reading Feminist Writing*, 162–203. New York: Columbia University Press, 1988.

Mini, Anne A. A. "An Expressive Revolution: The Political Theory of Germaine de Staël." Ph.D. diss., University of Washington, 1995.

————. "Reconstructing a Past in the Image of the Future: Mme de Stael's Re-conception of the French Revolutionary Identity." Presented at the Western Political Science Association Conference, Albuquerque, N.M. 1994.

Nietzsche, Friedrich. *The Gay Science.* Translated by Walter Kaufman. New York: Vintage, 1974.

Nussbaum, Martha. *The Fragility of Goodness: Luck and Ethics in Greek Tragedy and Philosophy.* Cambridge: Cambridge University Press, 1986.

————. *Love's Knowledge: Essays on Philosophy and Literature.* New York: Oxford University Press, 1990.

Okin, Susan. *Women in Western Political Thought.* Princeton: Princeton University Press, 1979.

Orlie, Melissa A. "Thoughtless Assertion and Political Deliberation." *American Political Science Review* 88, no. 3 (September 1994): 684–95.

Pateman, Carole. *The Disorder of Women.* Stanford, Calif.: Stanford University Press, 1989.

————. *The Sexual Contract.* Stanford, Calif.: Stanford University Press, 1988.

Plato. *The Republic.* Translated by G. M. A. Grube. Indianapolis: Hackett, 1992.

Rawls, John. *Political Liberalism.* New York: Columbia University Press, 1993.

————. *A Theory of Justice.* Oxford: Oxford University Press, 1971.

Riley, Denise. *"Am I That Name?" Feminism and the Category of 'Women' in History.* Minneapolis: University of Minnesota Press, 1988.

Rubin, Gayle. "The Traffic in Women: Notes on the 'Political Economy' of Sex." In *Toward an Anthropology of Women.* Edited by R. R. Reiter. New York: Monthly Review Press, 1975.

Ruddick, Sara. *Maternal Thinking: Towards a Politics of Peace.* New York: Ballantine 1989.

Sandel, Michael. *Liberalism and the Limits of Justice.* Cambridge: Cambridge University Press, 1982.

Sapiro, Virginia. "When are Interests Interesting? The Problem of Political Representation of Women." *American Political Science Review* 75 (September 1981): 717–21.

Schwartz, Joel. *The Sexual Politics of Jean-Jacques Rousseau.* Chicago: University of Chicago Press, 1984.

Scott, Joan Wallach. *Only Paradoxes to Offer: French Feminists and the Rights of Man.* Cambridge: Harvard University Press, 1996.

———. "A Woman Who has Only Paradoxes to Offer: Olympe de Gouges Claims Rights for Women." In *Rebel Daughters: Women and the French Revolution.* Edited by Sara E. Melzer and Leslie W. Rabine, 102–20. New York: Oxford University Press, 1992.

Sennett, Richard. *The Fall of Public Man.* New York: Vintage, 1974.

Showalter, English Jr. "Corinne as an Autonomous Heroine." In *Germaine de Staël: Crossing the Borders.* Edited by Madelyn Gutwirth, Avriel Goldberger, and Karyna Szmurlo, 188–92. New Brunswick, N.J.: Rutgers University Press, 1991.

Sklar, Judith. *Men and Citizens.* Cambridge: Cambridge University Press, 1969.

Spelman, Elizabeth. *Inessential Woman: Problems of Exclusion in Feminist Thought.* Boston: Beacon Press, 1988.

Starobinski, Jean. *Jean-Jacques Rousseau: Transparency and Obstruction.* Translated by Arthur Goldhammer. Chicago: University of Chicago Press, 1988.

———. "Suicide et melancolie chez Mme de Staël." *Preuves* 190, no. 16 (1966): 41–48.

Taylor, Charles. *Philosophy and the Human Sciences,* Philosophical Papers 2. Cambridge: Cambridge University Press, 1985.

Tenenbaum, Susan. "The Coppet Circle: Literary Criticism as Political Discourse." *History of Political Thought* 1, no. 3 (1980): 453–73.

———. "Liberal Heroines: Mme de Staël on the <<Woman question>> and the Modern State." *Annales Benjamin Constant* 5 (1985): 37–52.

Tronto, Joan C. *Moral Boundaries: A Political Argument for an Ethic of Care.* New York: Routledge, 1993.

Villemain, Abel François. *Cours de la littérature française; tableau de la littérature au XVIIIe siécle,* 4 vols. Paris: Perrin, 1891.

Walzer, Michael. *Spheres of Justice.* New York: Basic Books, 1983.

Weiss, Penny A. *Gendered Community: Rousseau, Sex, and Politics.* New York: New York University Press, 1993.

Wingrove, Elizabeth. "Sexual Performance as Political Performance in the *Lettre À M. D'Alembert Sur Les Spectacles.*" *Political Theory* 23, no. 4 (November 1995): 585–616.

Wohl, Victoria. "Exchange, Gender, and Subjectivity." In *Intimate Commerce.* Austin: University of Texas Press, 1998.

Young, Christine. *Configurations of Masculinity: A Feminist Perspective on Modern Political Theory.* Ithaca: Cornell University Press, 1991.

Young, Iris Marion. "Impartiality and the Civic Public: Some Implications of Feminist Critiques of Moral and Political Theory." In *Feminism As Critique.* Edited by Seyla Benhabib and Drucilla Cornell, 57–76. Minneapolis: University of Minnesota Press, 1987.

———. *Justice and the Politics of Difference.* Princeton: Princeton University Press, 1990.

Zerilli, Linda M. G. *Signifying Woman: Culture and Chaos in Rousseau, Burke, and Mill.* Ithaca: Cornell University Press, 1994.

Library of Congress Cataloging-in-Publication Data
Marso, Lori Jo.
  (Un)Manly citizens : Jean-Jacques Rousseau's and Germaine de
Staël's subversive women / Lori Jo Marso.
      p.   cm.
  Includes bibliographical references and index.
  ISBN 0-8018-6032-6 (alk. paper)
    1. Rousseau, Jean-Jacques, 1712–1778—Criticism and
interpretation. 2. Rousseau, Jean-Jacques, 1712–1778—Characters
—Women. 3. Staël, Madame de (Anne-Louise-Germaine), 1766–1817—
Criticism and interpretation. 4. Staël, Madame de (Anne-Louise-
Germaine), 1766–1817—Characters—Women. 5. Women in literature.
6. Citizenship in literature. 7. Feminism and literature.
I. Title.
PQ2053.M28   1999   98-36624
840.9'005—dc21   CIP

DATE DUE